AN ARTIST YOU DON'T HAVE TO BE!

A JEWISH ARTS AND CRAFTS BOOK

Written and Illustrated by
Joann Magnus with Howard I. Bogot

UAHC PRESS • NEW YORK, NEW YORK

Library of Congress Cataloging-in-Publication Data

Magnus, Joann.
    An artist you don't have to be! : a Jewish arts and crafts book /
Joann Magnus, Howard I. Bogot; illustrated by Joann Magnus.
      p. cm.
    ISBN 0–8074–0422–5
    1. Jewish crafts. 2. Judaism—Customs and practices. I. Bogot,
Howard. II. Title.
    BM729.H35M34 1990
    296.6′8—dc20   90–11023
                                      CIP

To those of you who are all heart and all thumbs. This book is meant to guide you through the world of Jewish arts and crafts, painlessly and joyfully.

Joann Magnus

To Lester J. Tanner for whom law is an art.
Howard I. Bogot

Why? What? How?

AN INTRODUCTION FOR PARENTS, TEACHERS, CAMP COUNSELORS: LOVERS OF JUDAISM AND ART

The starting point for the use of this book is a decision by a parent, teacher, camp counselor, or any individual to participate in a Jewish subject by means of a creative, artistic activity. Using this resource is comparable to using a cookbook as a guide to prepare a meal.

After you choose a Jewish subject, you will find it helpful to ask a series of questions concerning the arts-and-crafts recipes included in the category you've chosen: Why am I doing this project? Is it to provide myself or others with a fun experience? Am I trying to create something that is a useful product? Do I hope to encourage the development of new skills? Is this arts-and-crafts project designed to introduce a unique artistic style? How can this artistic experience enhance appreciation of and participation in Jewish life?

Answers to these questions may help you decide which of the projects featuring your chosen subject are the ones to consider.

If you are interested in a fun experience, choose instructions that sound like they will be relaxing and easy. Choose a project that doesn't demand a well-defined result and uses interesting media and materials that do not present too many technical challenges.

If you would like the arts-and-crafts experience to result in something useful, look for instructions that will result in a finished product either that is decorative or that has an efficient application to your daily life (e.g., a dining-table centerpiece or a bookmark).

If your answer to the question "Why do it?" is that you and the individuals with whom you are working desire to develop new skills, then choose those arts-and-crafts recipes included within your Jewish subject of interest that involve the most experimentation, either with media or technique. Look for a project in which participants can develop a sense of mastery as well as exhibit originality.

Your interest in artistic style should lead you to choose those projects that will enhance appreciation for a special approach to art by comparing the specified techniques with those used by influential artists of either the past or present.

Many of you readers will choose one or more arts-and-crafts projects within a Jewish subject category because you feel it will be an enriching Jewish life activity. If this is the reason for the choice, and an answer to the question "Why do it?," make sure as you proceed with the project that you have an opportunity to use your creativity in an actual Jewish life experience. For example—if you create a mezuzah, be sure to place it on the doorpost of a Jewish home or activity center along with an appropriate ceremony. If you design a bookcover, use it to enhance the elegance of a prayer book or haggadah as part of your or your family's regular use.

The second question you should ask yourself when using an arts-and-crafts recipe in this book is: When, where, and how will this project be developed? This question requires sensitivity to the size of the group involved in the process, the time given for participating in the arts-and-crafts project, the project's age appropriateness, and the setting in which the arts-and-crafts project takes place.

The size of the group will dictate such considerations as how long it will take to distribute the necessary supplies, how much supervision participants will need, and what effect size will have on the quality of the group experience. Members of a large group have very little chance to get to know one another or help one another complete a project, as some of the arts-and-crafts recipes suggest. A very small group, on the other hand, may be so competitive, in terms of artistic outcome, that certain projects should not be chosen.

When you choose a project from this book, be concerned with how much time you're allotting to the activity. Be sure you include time for both preparing and cleaning up the space, working with individuals, having participants share their work at different stages, and determining when the successful completion of the project has taken place.

Age appropriateness sounds very technical, yet some very basic age-related considerations can help determine the degree of success you and others experience when working on one or more of the arts-and-crafts recipes. For example, very young children, and some individuals, regardless of age, have great difficulty in what is often called hand/eye coordination and find it taxing and often frustrating to cut along a straight line or create complicated designs. Such people work better with large movements of the hands and arms. They see things in broad brush strokes rather than in intricate patterns.

Attention span is also an important concern. If a project takes too long before the "artist" can see some results, boredom can destroy enjoyment and fulfillment. Take a look at the recipe, and determine how long it will take for completion, then consider the people participating in the project and decide whether or not their patience merits the choice you have made.

Parents, teachers, and camp counselors might also find it important to consider whether members of the group will be comfortable or uncomfortable with the smell, touch, and sight of the different media involved in a project. For example, using wet, squishy materials can be a very negative experience for some people. If this type of response seems probable, choose another project or adapt the instructions to substitute materials that are more acceptable to the people involved.

We also suggest you choose a project recipe in which the outcomes will motivate the participants. For instance: choose a project that could result in a wall display for school, home, or camp cabin; a gift that can be given to a friend or family member; a product that can be sold to earn funds to benefit people in need; or a group project for a stage-set design many audiences will appreciate.

One last aspect to consider in choosing a project involves the setting in which the arts-and-crafts activity takes place.

If the workplace is at home, will you choose a project that can be done by the entire family, or will it be a project for just one individual? If you are choosing a project for use at camp, will the project work best with a cabin group, a division of campers, a specialized arts-and-crafts workshop, or with one or more campers during their leisure time?

If school is the setting for the arts-and-crafts activity, perhaps you can choose a recipe within your topic of interest that will involve the entire school community. Some projects will work best in the classroom, others in an assembly designed for schoolmates close in age, while some are perfect opportunities for a student to become involved in an independent study project.

We believe most of the arts-and-crafts projects included in this book can be adapted and used in a variety of ways.

Feel free to revise any recipe so it fills the precise needs you have identified.

Thank You

A very special thank you to Phyllis Bentley; Rabbi Marc Gruber; the many Eisner Camp Institute Art Shack campers; students at Solomon Schechter Day School in Jericho, Long Island; my children, Jennifer and Adam; and my "almost" children, Mara, Aaron, Rebecca, Cory, Lisa, and Adina—all of whom donated ideas and the willingness to try any and all art projects I asked them to do. Without them these projects wouldn't have come to life. To my husband, Allen, who tolerated my compulsive need to collect "treasures" for my many art projects in our overcrowded garage, an acknowledgment of both appreciation and love. For all their help in putting together a front cover that reflects this book, a thank you and a kiss to Martin Weiss for photographing the group, and to Allen Magnus, Jennifer Magnus, Adam Magnus, Hope Zimmerman, Daniel Zimmerman, Rebecca Zimmerman, Renee Shellock, Susan Weiss, Betsy Leff, Austin Leff, and Jody Weinberg for giving up a sunny afternoon in March to "pose." A lot of people and love created this book. Thanks! Some of the projects in this book originally appeared in *Shofar* magazine in the author's "Creative You" column.

Joann Magnus

Creative thinking, experience, and expression have always been hallmarks of Jewish survival. My words of appreciation are, therefore, focused on Jewish ancestors, and those Jews who exist at the present time. Their dreams have always made me feel like a singer, dancer, poet, and sculptor even though my skills were those of the amateur.

Overwhelming thanks, however, belong to those children whose drawings and poetry fill the pages of the text *I Never Saw Another Butterfly: Children's Drawings and Poems from Theresienstadt Concentration Camp, 1942–1944*. The traced hand of a child destroyed by hate touches the title page with an energy we are obligated to embrace. Those children were not artists, and we need not be artists in order to gift wrap Judaism with ribbons of rainbows.

Howard I. Bogot

Contents

TU BISHVAT

VALUES

YOM HASHOAH/KRISTALLNACHT

YOM KIPPUR

APPENDIX

Moses Umbrella Puppet

OBJECTIVES:

To learn about Moses.

To create a puppet from a throwaway umbrella.

To create a biography of Moses to use in a puppet presentation.

MATERIALS:

Old umbrella, large Styrofoam ball four-inch circumference* (three-inch or five-inch is good too), yarn, cotton, buttons or wiggly eyes,* red felt, black magic marker, square of white fabric or man's white felt handkerchief, piece of felt* (for hands), glue, scissors. *(These supplies can be found in any arts-and-crafts, hobby, or five-and-ten-cent store.)

DIRECTIONS:

1. Remove all but two of the metal spires of an old, broken umbrella. Have an adult do this: it can be tricky. These spires will become the arms of Moses.

2. For his head you will need a large Styrofoam ball. Push it onto the point at the top of the umbrella. (See Figure A.)

3. Use yarn or cotton for hair and a beard, wiggly eyes or buttons for eyes, and red felt for lips. Glue them all on. For the headpiece use a square of fabric or a man's handkerchief. Place it on the head, and tie a cord around the forehead. Add felt hands to the tip of the spines, and Moses is ready to speak to the Hebrews. (See Figure B.)

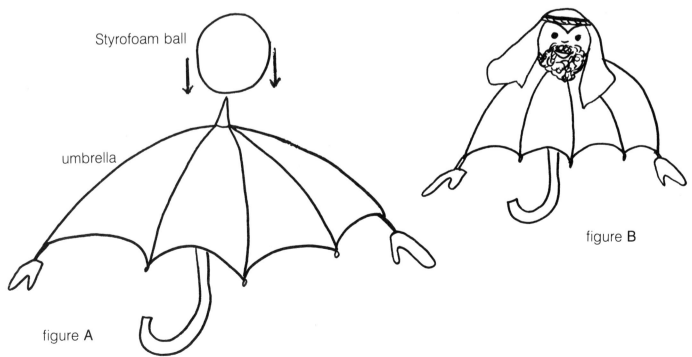

figure A   figure B

2 "And Then There Was Light" Interpretive Collage

OBJECTIVES: To create a modern and personal midrash from a biblical passage.
To create a black-and-white torn-paper collage describing Genesis 1:3.

MATERIALS: Twelve-by-eighteen-inch black-and-white construction paper, glue, copy of Genesis 1:1–4.

DIRECTIONS:
1. Read the biblical passage several times. Formulate in your own mind how this "light" might have appeared.

2. Using the black paper as the background, tear the white paper to fit into your idea of what the "light" looked like in Genesis 1:3. The white paper can be folded, twisted, or torn.

3. Glue the white paper onto the black paper.

4. *Optional*—On an index card write in one sentence what your idea of the "light" was about. Staple at the bottom of your collage.

Twelve Hebrew Tribes "Stained Glass" Pictures/Windows

In ancient Israel, according to tradition, the Jewish people consisted of twelve tribes, named after the twelve sons of Jacob. The twelve tribes were: Reuben, Simeon, Levi, Judah, Issachar, Zebulun, Dan, Naphtali, Gad, Asher, Joseph (Ephraim and Manasseh, his sons), and Benjamin. Each tribe had its own symbol, e.g., Judah—lion; Dan—scale; Zebulun—double-sail ship; Joseph—bale of wheat. (All the symbols are on the sides of a box of Chanukah candles from Ner-Zion factory.)

OBJECTIVES:

To familiarize students with the names and symbols of the twelve tribes of Israel.
To create mock "stained glass" windows.

MATERIALS:

Pictures and names of the twelve tribes of Israel, permanent magic markers, clear acetate sheets (eight-and-a-half-by-eleven inches, or five-by-seven inches), drawing paper same size as acetate sheets, paper clips, tape, pencil. (If acetate sheets are unavailable from an arts-and-crafts store, scrap pieces of lamination material are acceptable. Clear scrap lamination paper can be obtained from any Board of Jewish Education where lamination of paper or posters is done or any store that laminates posters or any museum that mounts them.)

DIRECTIONS:

1. Cut twelve pieces of drawing paper the same size as the acetate sheets.

2. Draw the symbol for each tribe and the name of the tribe lengthwise on the paper. Do one sheet for each of the twelve tribes.

3. Place the acetate on top of the drawing and paper-clip it in place.

4. Using the permanent magic markers, copy the design on the acetate sheets. Color in the background and the drawing with the markers.

5. Remove the drawing paper.

6. Hang the twelve pictures on a window so the light can shine through the mock "stained glass" windows.

Noah's Ark with Cookie Puppets

OBJECTIVES:
To create Noah's ark.
To create animal puppets on a stick for the ark.
To study Genesis 6:1–22.

MATERIALS:
A box of animal crackers, ice cream sticks or pencils, wiggly eyes or tiny buttons, magic markers, yarn, pipe cleaners, one sheet of newspaper (the largest you can find), glue, four large paper clips, clear varnish spray or hair spray. (Wiggly eyes, pipe cleaners, and ice cream sticks can be purchased in an arts-and-crafts or fabric store.)

DIRECTIONS:

1. Decorate the animal crackers so they look special. Use yarn, buttons, or anything you think will make the animals look great. Use the glue to put on decorations. Spray the crackers. Remember to spray away from your face.

2. Glue the animals onto the top of the sticks. Make many animals.

3. For the ark: Take the sheet of newspaper and fold it in half (see Figure A). Next fold in each corner on the top until it looks like Figure B. Glue the folds in position. Secure them with paper clips while they dry. Then fold the bottom half up. Let it just cover the corners you just folded. It will look like Figure C. Do this in the front and the back. The last two folds (see Figure D) make the ark a real boat shape. Hold these folds with glue and paper clips. Remove the paper clips when the glue has dried.

4. Place your puppets in the ark and sing "Rise and Shine" while moving the ark.

. . . .

THE ARK

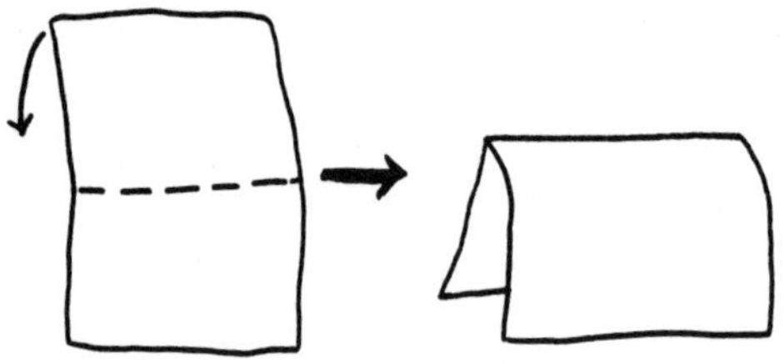

figure C

figure A

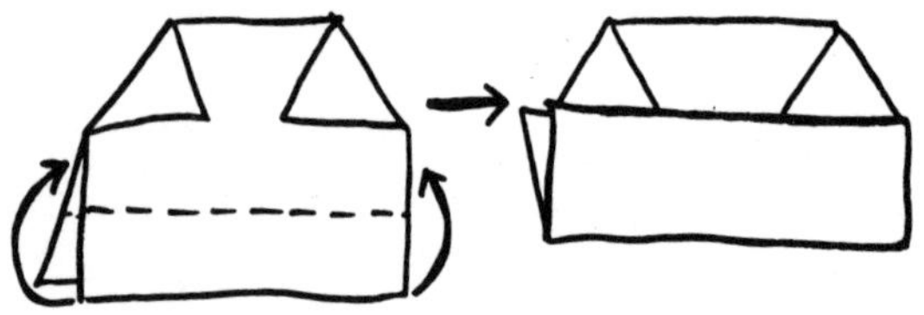

figure B

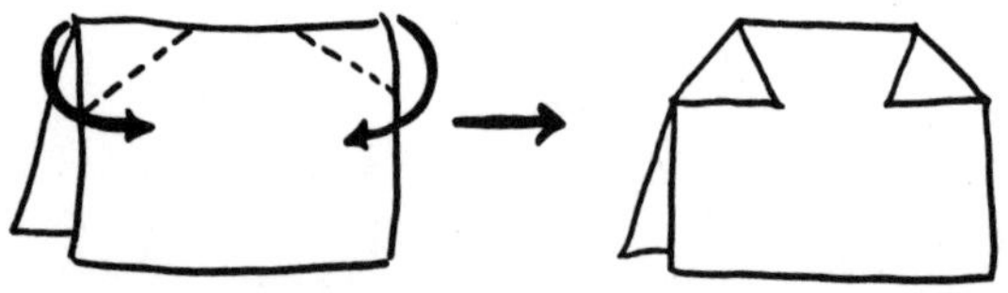

figure D

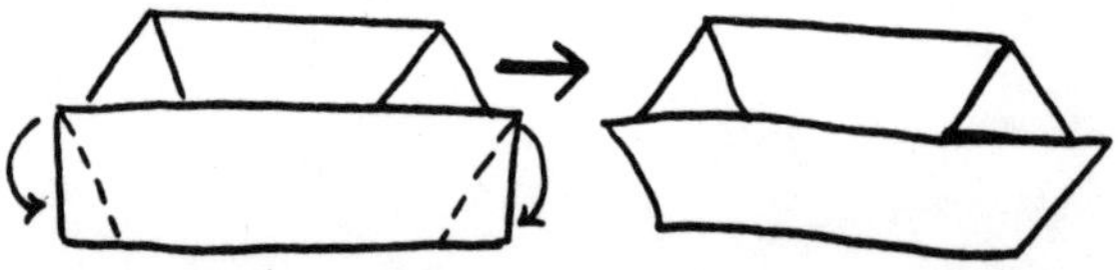

OBJECTIVES:

To pick a moment in the Bible of historical value and "freeze-frame" it in time.
To create these moments using figures made from aluminum foil figures covered in plaster strips.

MATERIALS:

Plaster of paris strips (the kind used in setting broken limbs and bought at an arts-and-crafts or medical supply store), scissors, heavy-gauge (duty) aluminum foil, an empty shoebox, watercolor paints, spray shellac or clear varnish.

DIRECTIONS:

1. Tear a strip of aluminum foil. Twisting it, form it into the shape of the character you are representing in your frozen "moment" in biblical time. Several pieces may be necessary to form the figure.

2. Staple the feet to the "bottom" of the shoebox (which you have turned upside down).

3. Fill a bowl with warm water. Cut the plaster of paris strips into pieces three to four inches long. Dip into the water, and cover the foil character with the wet strip. Smooth down the strip. Keep covering the foil until no foil shows. Let dry.

4. Make sure your character looks as if it were frozen in the middle of an action.

5. You can add additional characters if they are a part of the historical "moment."

6. Mountains, trees, rocks can also be added using the same plaster-strip-covered–foil method.

7. When dry, either spray with the varnish or paint in with the watercolors. Your moment in history has now come alive!

6 Paper Chanukah Puppets

OBJECTIVES: To study the Chanukah drama.

To act out the story of Chanukah.

Toeate folded paper puppets.

MATERIALS: Nine-by-twelve-inch heavy drawing paper, magic markers, yarn, buttons, glue, scissors.

DIRECTIONS:
1. Fold the drawing paper the long way (see Figure A).

2. Now fold the paper in half again, the short way this time (see Figure B).

3. Now you have a "book" shape. Crease the "covers" on lines A and B, and fold them according to Figure C.

4. If you hold the paper in a "standing up" position, you will have a puppet. Put your thumb in the bottom pocket and your index finger in the top pocket. There's a mouth in the middle. Make it talk by opening and closing your fingers. Tape it if the puppet is sliding off your hand (see Figure D).

5. Decorate the top of the puppet with yarn, button eyes, curled paper, magic marker. Your puppet can look like Judah the Maccabee; Mattathias, his father; or Hannah, a brave Hebrew woman.

. . . .

CHANUKAH PUPPET

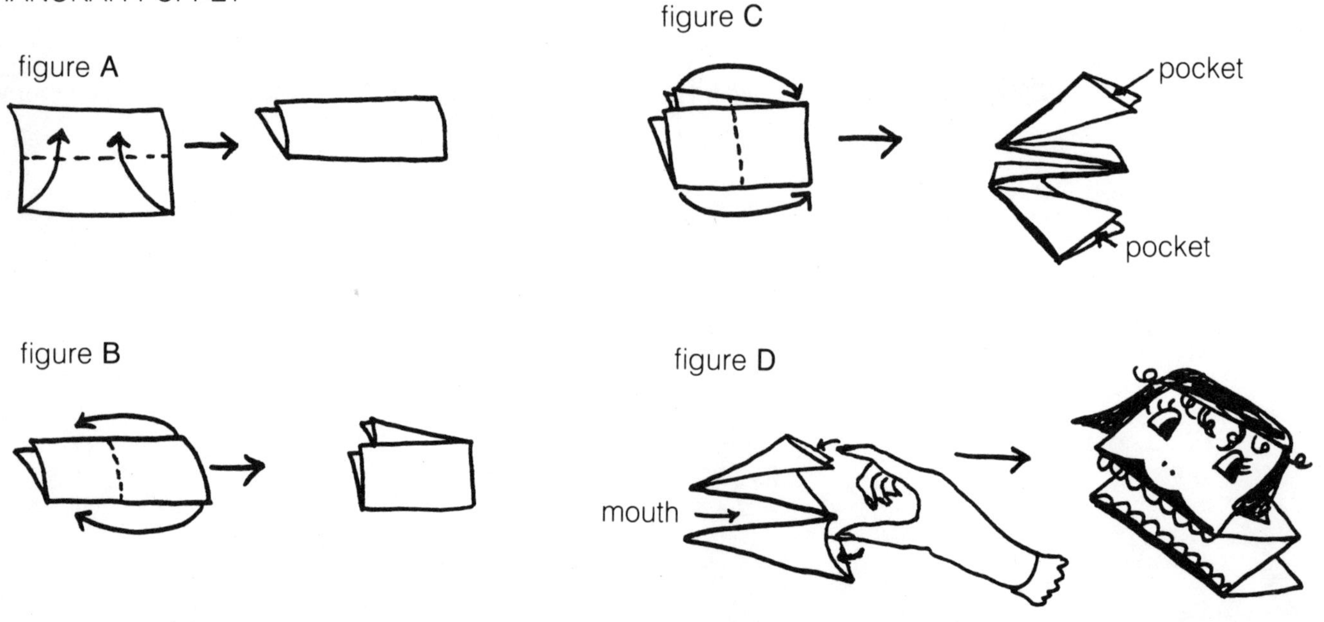

figure **A**

figure **C**

pocket

pocket

figure **B**

figure **D**

mouth

Chanukah "Rubbings" Gift Wrap Paper

OBJECTIVE: To make wrapping paper for Chanukah gift wrapping.

MATERIALS: Sheets of large white paper (plain white gift wrap tissue, butcher paper, watercolor paper, or thin drawing paper are all good), crayons, oaktag (or shirt cardboard), Chanukah symbol patterns (see Appendix for patterns), scissors.

DIRECTIONS:

1. Peel the paper from the crayons.

2. Cut out and place the patterns found in the Appendix on the oaktag and cut out. Place these oaktag patterns under the white paper.

3. Rub the crayons back and forth over the top of the white paper where the oaktag pattern is underneath. Rub until the crayon pattern emerges.

4. Keep placing the patterns all around the paper until you have filled it up with beautiful rubbings of Chanukah symbols.

Chanukah "Stained Glass" Cookie Mobile

OBJECTIVES:
To create a mobile using symbols of Chanukah.
To learn how to make "stained glass" cookies.

MATERIALS:
Aluminum foil, cookie sheets, straw, sugar cookie dough (see Appendix for recipe), one bag of lollipops, knife, hanger, yarn, one large white paper plate, Chanukah symbols, cookie cutters or patterns (see Appendix). (Cookie cutters can be bought in a Judaic shop or the baking supply section of a standard shop.)

DIRECTIONS:

1. Make the cookie dough according to the recipe in the Appendix or use your own favorite cookie recipe. (It should roll out easily.) Using the cookie cutters or the patterns found in the Appendix (trace the patterns onto oaktag and use the oaktag patterns to cut the shapes from the dough), cut out the Chanukah cookies.

2. Using the knife, cut out squares or rectangular shapes in the cookie dough. It should look like the patterns in a stained glass window.

3. Put a hole with a straw in the top of the cookie to hang it. Place the cut-out patterned dough on a foil-covered cookie sheet.

4. Place the lollipops (only the pop not the stick) in a brown bag, and crush them with a hard object. Keep the colors separate.

5. Sprinkle the crushed lollipops into the cutouts in the cookie. Bake according to directions. DO NOT OVERBAKE!

6. When cool, put a twelve-inch piece of yarn through the hole in the cookie.

7. Attach all the cookies, at varying lengths, to the bottom of the hanger.

8. Make a small hole in the center of the paper plate and put it over the hanger. Fold the plate in half, and staple the sides together over the hanger. Write the word "Chanukah" on the plate. Hang the mobile up in a window so the sun can shine through the "stained glass" cookie.

Chanukah Dreidels

OBJECTIVE: To make dreidels from egg cartons.

MATERIALS: Paper egg cartons (Styrofoam are usable but not as good as paper egg cartons), magic markers, a sharpened orange stick (a sharpened pencil like a golf pencil can be used also).

DIRECTIONS:
1. Cut out the egg cup section of the egg carton.

2. Put the orange stick through the center (see Figure A) with the point down.

3. Using the magic marker, draw the Hebrew letters *nun*, *gimel*, *hei*, and *shin* on four sides of the cup section. These stand for *"Nes Gadol Hayah Sham"* (A Great Miracle Happened There).

4. Twirl the pencil, and watch the dreidel spin.

. . . .

DREIDEL

figure **A**

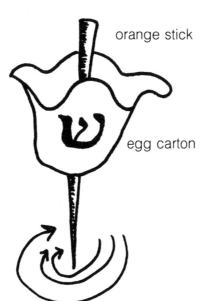

orange stick

egg carton

10   A Chanukah Microtopography Picture

Jews have often developed unique art forms to decorate their precious books. A long time ago Jews decorated their siddurim and haggadot with tiny words forming beautiful shapes, designs, and realistic forms. These tiny words were often descriptive of what they formed. Sometimes they were prayers or stories forming images of what they referred to.

OBJECTIVE: To make a microtopography picture using symbols associated with Chanukah.

MATERIALS: Drawing paper twelve-by-eighteen inches or larger, narrow-pointed magic markers, pencils, picture frame.

DIRECTIONS:
1. Draw a thin pencil-line design as a guide for the tiny words. Pictures of Chanukah symbols, the words "shalom," "Maccabee," "candles," and "chanukiah" (a Chanukah menorah) are wonderful ideas for the picture.

2. Using tiny words representing the area drawn or the word itself, such as "shalom," create an overall design with magic markers. For example, a picture of the candles in the Chanukah menorah (chanukiah) can be drawn and the word "flame" drawn repeatedly in the shape of flames, the word "candle" for the candles, etc. These can be done in an outline or a completely filled-in design.

3. Mount and frame.

Cup People Name Settings for Shabbat, Passover, or Shavuot

OBJECTIVES: To create "living" place settings.

To make our special meal for Shabbat, Passover, or Shavuot (or any holiday) creative and personal.

MATERIALS: Seven-ounce white Styrofoam hot cups (one for each member of your family), planting soil to fill each cup, one cup of grass seeds, magic markers.

DIRECTIONS:

1. Using your markers, draw eyes, a nose, and a mouth on each cup. Write each person's name at the top or the bottom of the cup.

2. Fill the cup (almost to the top) with the soil. Pat it down. Sprinkle a tablespoonful of grass seed on top.

3. Water the seeds and soil. Place the cup in a sunny spot. The grass will grow and look like the cup person's hair. Place each cup on your table for Shabbat, Passover, or Shavuot as a place setting.

The Making of a Family Torah

OBJECTIVES: To make a family Torah.
To appreciate the importance our family has to us.
To work together on a project.

MATERIALS: Two dowels or toilet paper tubes to be used as rollers, a long piece of drawing paper to be the actual "Torah," a nine-by-twelve-inch piece of felt, aluminum foil for the crown and *yad*, a square of art foil for the breastplate, glue, sequins, trim, yarn, permanent magic markers.

DIRECTIONS:

1. Draw, using markers or crayons, "What is important to me." Have each member of your family do the same on the paper.

2. Color in the rollers or tubes with markers or crayons and attach the paper to them. Roll them toward the middle, and attach a paper clip to hold it in place.

3. Wrap the felt around the rolled-up paper and dowels. Glue in the back to hold it as a cover for the Torah. Decorate with the trim, buttons, and sequins.

4. Cut a square from the art foil and punch a hole in each corner. Attach a piece of yarn to each hole and hang off the dowels. Decorate the breastplate with permanent markers.

5. Roll a small piece of aluminum foil into a *yad* shape and tie a piece of yarn around the top. Hang off the dowel.

6. Cut a piece of art foil into the shape of a crown and color with the permanent markers. Bend around the top of the dowels as a crown.

Art Foil Mezuzah

OBJECTIVE: To make a mezuzah out of art foil.

MATERIALS: Art foil, permanent magic markers, pencil, scissors, paper (calligraphy pen and parchment if the scroll is also to be made).

DIRECTIONS:

1. Distribute drawing paper and pencil. Design a mezuzah on the paper. Designs can be cut and shaped to see if you have a feasible design. Some ideas that are interesting for a foil mezuzah include: a Noah's ark, a flame, the tablets, an envelope shape, an *Aron Hakodesh*, a rectangle design.

2. Cut the foil to fit the paper design. Bend and cut where your design indicates. Watch out for sharp cuts.

3. Draw the symbols and design on the foil so an impression occurs. Don't forget to include a *shin* in the mezuzah design or the word *"Shaddai"* to the design.

4. Color the mezuzah with permanent magic markers.

5. You can write out the *Shema* and the *Ve'ahavta* on a piece of parchment and place it in the back, or you can purchase a kosher scroll in any Judaic store.

6. The mezuzah can be nailed to the doorpost.

14   Dor L'Dor Generational Collage

Dor l'dor means "from generation to generation." The generations that came before us have in so many ways enriched our lives. In each of our families we have pictures, recipes, mementos, clothing, ritual items, books, or other items that belonged to or had meaning for our parents or grandparents.

OBJECTIVES: To collect pictures, etc., that are a part of our family's history and make them into a collage.

To make a *dor l'dor* collage.

MATERIALS: Eighteen-by-twenty-four-inch piece of heavy cardboard (can be larger), glue, scissors, can of varnish or clear shellac, pictures, pieces of ribbon, doilies, magazine pictures of things that were a part of what your parents or grandparents liked or that represented something in their lives. Copies of favorite recipes that have been passed down from generation to generation.

DIRECTIONS:
1. Gather all your bits and pieces for your collage. If necessary, take a Polaroid snapshot of anything that cannot be glued onto the cardboard for the collage.

2. Glue all the items onto the cardboard.

3. Spray the collage with the shellac or the varnish.

4. Write the words *"dor l'dor"* at the top of the collage (or anywhere else on the collage).

NOTE: A collage is a picture of many different pieces. It can also include many different textures and media. When glued together, it forms one whole picture of many different items.

Replica of an Ancient Clay Name Stamp

In ancient times scribes would send their messages etched in clay. Each scribe or citizen would have his or her own personal seal or stamp. This stamp is very much like the modern-day name and address labels we affix to envelopes.

OBJECTIVES: To create a replica of an ancient name stamp.
To practice using modern and ancient Hebrew alphabets.

MATERIALS: Five-by-three-inch slab of self-hardening (or firing) clay, a pencil or orange stick, a five-by-three-inch piece of thin white paper for drawing (ditto paper is fine), additional clay for later use. (Clay can be bought in a hobby, arts-and-crafts, or ceramic shop.)

DIRECTIONS:
1. On the white paper write your last name in English. Keep the lettering simple and at least one inch high.

2. Write the Hebrew spelling of your last name under the English spelling, also making it at least one inch high.

3. *Optional*—Under the modern Hebrew spelling one of the ancient Hebrew alphabets can be used. The *Encyclopaedia Judaica* has various scripts.

4. Put the drawing paper up to a window so the letters appear reversed on the back of the paper. Trace, using the pencil, the reversed version of your name. You will need to write all lettering upon the clay in its backward form. When you press the hardened clay into fresh clay, your name will then appear correctly.

5. Lay the backward lettering upon the five-by-three-inch clay slab. Trace with a pencil or orange stick. Make sure to press deeply so the lettering will appear upon the clay slab. Remove the paper and straighten out the lettering so it is neat and clear to read. (Remember it will all be in reverse, even the Hebrew!) Symbolic drawings can be added now.

6. Let the clay dry (or fire it). When hardened, press into soft clay and your name will appear raised and correctly.

16   Paint-on-Wax Hebrew Letters (Wax-Resist)

December 12 is the birthday of Eliezer Ben-Yehuda (1858–1922), known as the "father of modern Hebrew." In his honor let's make great-looking Hebrew letters to decorate our home and classroom.

OBJECTIVES:

To create Hebrew letters from wax-resist techniques.
To decorate the home, classroom, and sukah.

MATERIALS:

Three or four pieces of oaktag nine-by-twelve inches, three (or more) colors of tempera paint, paintbrushes for each color, a wax Sabbath candle (white), a pencil, scissors, newspaper to work on.

DIRECTIONS:

1. With the pencil, outline Hebrew letters (the Hebrew months, days, words, your name, holiday names, colors) on the oaktag. Make them big and wide, at least eight inches high and four inches wide.

2. Fill in each letter with the wax from the white candle. Make sure the whole letter space is filled in with wax markings. You can fill it in with a solid line or a line design.

3. Using the tempera paint, color the letters. The tempera paint will stick only to the oaktag that has no wax on it. The paint will "bubble up" on the waxed section. This is known as wax-resist technique.

4. Using the scissors, *after* the paint dries, cut out each Hebrew letter.

5. Hang or tape the letters up in order.

Ceramic Hebrew/English Name Door Plaque

At birth each child is given a Hebrew name as well as a civil (English) name. There are two conflicting customs about choosing an appropriate name for a baby. The Ashkenazic custom is to name a child in memory of someone who has died. The Sephardic custom is to name a child in honor of a living relative.

OBJECTIVES:

To create a ceramic name door plaque.

To illustrate our Hebrew name according to its meaning/symbolism.

MATERIALS:

Ceramic tile (from tile store) six-by-six inches or six-by-three inches or any suitable size, one plastic picture hanger, glue, permanent magic markers (including gold or silver), sequins, beads, or trimmings.

DIRECTIONS:

1. Glue the picture hanger to the back of the tile. Let dry.

2. Write in gold or silver marker your English and/or Hebrew name on the tile.

3. Draw appropriate symbols to decorate the tile: e.g., Yonina—little dove, Devorah—bee, David—crown, Ari—lion, Dov—bear. (Consult a name guide such as "A Dictionary of Jewish Names" in *The Jewish Catalog I*.)

4. Glue on sequins, beads, or trimming to further decorate the name tile. Let dry. Hang on door.

Calligraphy in the Style of Michel Schwartz

Michel Schwartz is a renowned calligraphic artist who uses his extensive Torah knowledge to create works of art using key Hebrew words from the Torah.

OBJECTIVES:
To create a calligraphic work of art using key Hebrew words found in the Torah.
To create art in the artistic style of Michel Schwartz.

MATERIALS:
Nine-by-twelve-inch white drawing paper, pencil, magic markers.

DIRECTIONS:

1. Choose a word from the Torah—e.g., *bereshit*, shalom, *Yisrael*, Shabbat, *kadosh*, shofar, Sinai.

2. Lightly sketch a picture that symbolizes the Hebrew word, such as a dove for shalom, a ram's horn for shofar, a mountain for Sinai, the outline of Jerusalem for *Yisrael* (see Figure A).

3. Fit the Hebrew word (written in English or Hebrew) into the outline of the symbolic drawing (see Figure B).

4. Color in the letters with the markers.

. . . .

figure **A**

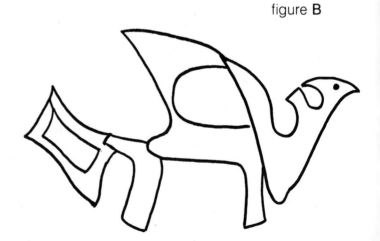

SHOFAR

figure **B**

שלום

Scratch Art Hebrew Letters

OBJECTIVES:
To create Hebrew letters from wax-resist techniques.
To decorate our home/classroom.

MATERIALS:
Three or four nine-by-twelve-inch pieces of oaktag, black poster paint or drawing ink, a paintbrush, a box of wax crayons, a pencil, scissors, newspapers to work on.

DIRECTIONS:

1. With the pencil, outline Hebrew letters (the Hebrew months, days, words of objects, your Hebrew name, holiday names, famous people's names) on the oaktag. Make them big and bold, at least eight inches high.

2. Color in each letter with the crayons. Fill in all the space. Put the colors on thickly. Use many colors on each Hebrew letter.

3. Cut the letters out and paint them all over with the black paint or ink. (Work on newspaper, please!)

4. Use the point of the scissors (carefully) or the handle of the paintbrush to scratch colored patterns and shapes in the black letters.

5. Hang or tape the letters up in order.

OBJECTIVES: To nominate Jewish historic figures to a "Jewish Hall of Fame."

To study famous figures to decide who will be nominated.

To create soft-sculpture cup people.

MATERIALS: A pair of old panty hose, cotton or pillow filler, a needle and thread, yarn or cotton for hair, fabric trim, buttons or wiggly eyes for the face, large Styrofoam cups, magic markers, five-by-seven-inch index cards, a piece of tape to hold the head in place. (Wiggly eyes can be purchased in an arts-and-crafts store or five-and-ten.)

DIRECTIONS:

1. Cut the feet off the panty hose. Make a ball shape from the leg. Stuff it full. This will be the head. Tie it at the neck (see Figure A).

2. Pull out a small nose from the center of the face. Thread a needle, and push it through the other side of the pulled-out nose. Push it through the other side of the nose again and then back again and again. Tie and cut the thread (see Figure B).

3. Glue the eyes on. Sew or glue on yarn or white cotton for hair. Draw a magic-marker mouth and cheeks. Trim the head to look like your hero/heroine.

4. Punch a small hole in the bottom of the cup and push the neck through. Tape the neck into the cup. Draw the body of your person on the cup. Write his or her name on a folded index card, and place it in front of the "cup" person (see Figure C).

5. Line up your nominees in a "Hall of Fame."

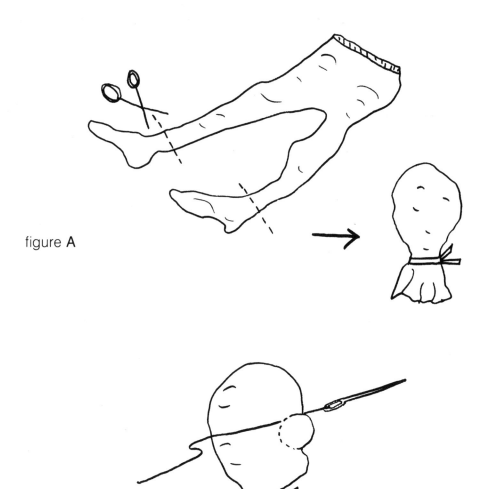

figure A

figure B

figure C

Israeli Map Cookie

OBJECTIVES: To recreate the country of Israel in an edible form.
To locate major cities and landmarks of Israel on a cookie map.

MATERIALS: Basic sugar cookie recipe (see Appendix for recipe), chocolate chips, food coloring, one egg yolk per color, brushes, cinnamon "hots" (candy buttons may be used instead), cardboard shape of Israel (see Appendix for shape), knife, baking cookie sheet.

DIRECTIONS:

1. Mix up cookie dough recipe. Roll out to one-quarter-inch thickness. (See Appendix.)

2. Place map-of-Israel shape onto cookie dough and cut around the edges.

3. Mix one egg yolk with several drops of color. Blue, yellow, and green are needed. Put a brush in each color (the egg yolk will turn the food coloring shiny when baked).

4. Referring to a simple map of Israel, mark off the major cities with the cinnamon "hots," the mountains with chocolate chips, the water areas with blue food coloring (apply with brush), the lush green areas with green food coloring, and the desert area with yellow food coloring.

5. Bake at suggested heat. Do not overbake. The cookie will look more colorful if it is underbaked.

Enjoy the land "flowing with milk and honey," chocolate chips, and cinnamon "hots."

Flag of Israel

The modern national flag of Israel, blue and white with the Magen David in the center, was adopted by the Zionists in 1898. It was conceived by David Wolffsohn and is reminiscent of the ritual prayer shawl, the talit.

OBJECTIVES:

To create a flag of Israel from paper or fabric.
To create a symbol of Israel.

MATERIALS:

Paper Flag—twelve-by-eighteen-inch white drawing paper or butcher paper, one-inch brush, blue paint, magic marker or eighteen-by-twenty-four-inch blue construction paper, glue, scissors, one-quarter-inch dowel (dowels can be purchased in arts-and-crafts or hobby shops, as well as in lumberyards).
Fabric Flag—one white pillowcase (will make two flags), blue tempera paint and one-inch wide paintbrush, twenty-four-by-eighteen-inch cardboard, ruler, X-acto knife, one-half-inch dowel, blue spray paint.

DIRECTIONS:

Paper Flag

1. Glue the flag to the dowel at the short side. Let dry.

2. Paint a stripe at both the top and bottom of the paper one-half inch from the edge, or cut two strips two-by-eighteen-inches from the construction paper, and glue the paper one-half inch from the top and bottom edges.

3. Paint a Magen David (see Figure A) in the middle of the flag, or cut six strips one-half-by-four inches from the blue construction paper. Form two triangles into a Magen David and glue onto paper. (Repeat on opposite side.)

Fabric Flag

1. Cut the pillowcase along the edges to form two flag shapes. (Repeat the following directions if you are making two flags.)

2. Glue short edge to the dowel. Let dry.

3. Place fabric on newspaper. Paint a stripe at top and bottom. Let dry. Paint a Magen David (see Figure A) in the center. Let dry and repeat on opposite side, or, in the middle of the cardboard rule a strip one-and-a-half-by-twenty-inches. Cut the strip out with the X-acto knife. Place the stencil so the strip is one inch from the top (and then the bottom). Cover the rest of the flag that is exposed with newspaper so it won't be splattered. Spray the stencil stripes. Then paint the Magen David in the middle. Repeat on the opposite side when the first side is dry.

. . . .

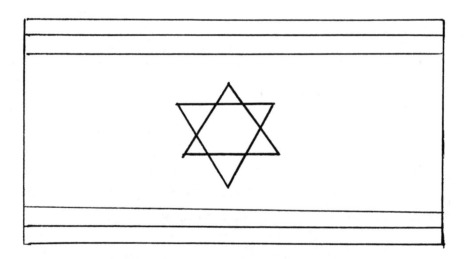

figure **A**

Snow (Sheleg) Pictures

The Hebrew word for snow is *"sheleg"* (שֶׁלֶג). Snow has fallen in Israel, especially in the northern areas and Jerusalem. Creating snow pictures is both fun and "feels" like what you are creating.

OBJECTIVES: To create "snow" pictures.
To learn the Hebrew word for snow.

MATERIALS: A box of Ivory Snow flakes, bowl, water, spoon, twelve-by-eighteen-inch dark piece of oaktag, pencil, spray shellac (or hair spray).

DIRECTIONS:

1. Draw an outline of the Jerusalem skyline two-thirds of the way up from the bottom of the oaktag. (Any skyline or simple outdoor scene is fine.)

2. Take a cup of Ivory Snow flakes and pour into a large bowl. Add enough water to make a thick mushy paste.

3. Use a spoon to put the snowflake mush onto a large twelve-by-eighteen-inch dark piece of drawing paper.

4. Create a snow scene by spreading out this mixture on your picture. Spray with hair spray or shellac to prevent crumbling.

Waving an Israeli Flag in Honor of Yom Ha'atzma'ut

Israel was declared an independent Jewish state on May 14, 1948.

To study the holiday of Yom Ha'atzma'ut.
To create, for fun, a person (or you) waving Israeli flags.

Cardboard or oaktag eight-and-a-half-by-eleven inches, pencil, scissors, one paper fastener, magic markers, eighteen-inch piece of yarn, two toothpicks, one piece of drawing paper or one index card.

1. Cut out the shape of your body and two arms. Poke a hole in the body and in each end of the arm. Cut out your face from a photograph and glue it onto the face (see Figure A).

2. To assemble, put a paper fastener through the hole in the body and attach the arms in the back. Close the fastener loosely so the arms move. Put the ends of the yarn through the hand holes and tie a knot (see Figure B).

3. Cut an index card in half and glue the toothpicks to the sides. Make two blue stripes and a Star of David on each. Glue the flags to the hands. Pull the yarn and wave the flags (see Figure C). (See Appendix for pattern.)

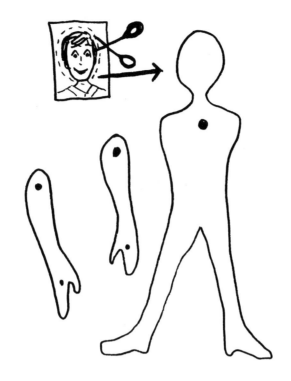

figure A

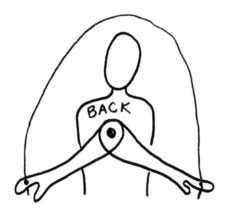

figure B

figure C

28   Israeli Desert Sand Painting

Much of Israel is desert, which includes the Aravah, the Judean Hills, and the Negev. The desert has its own quiet beauty, changing colors each hour.

OBJECTIVES: To create a desert scene using sand as paint so it feels as well as looks like a desert. To learn how to "paint" with sand.

MATERIALS: One-half pound of red, yellow, brown, white, beige, blue, and green sand, brush, glue, pencil, eighteen-by-twenty-four inch piece of cardboard, newspaper, spoon, can of spray varnish or polymer. (Colored sand can be purchased at any arts-and-crafts or hobby shop. Aquariums or tropical fish stores may carry it as well.)

DIRECTIONS:

1. Draw a simple scene of one of the Israeli deserts. (Look at photographs in books or travel brochures.) Keep it a simple line drawing.

2. Using the brush, spread glue on the top of the cardboard or "sky" section.

3. Gently tape the spoon of blue sand onto the glue. Lift the cardboard up and tip off any excess sand onto the paper.

4. Glue one color at a time, working from the top to the bottom and from one side to the other.

5. When glue is dry, spray with the shellac.

Multi-Image Picture of Israel in the Style of
Yaacov Agam

Yaacov Agam lives in Israel and creates works of art in many different media: paint, plastic, metal, clay, and stone. He often creates multi-image pictures by dividing his surface into "folds" and tucking his picture along these "folds."

OBJECTIVES:

To make a multi-image picture.

To replicate an artistic style.

To acquaint students with the works of Yaacov Agam.

MATERIALS:

White drawing paper (nine-by-twelve inches or twelve-by-eighteen inches or larger), glue, scissors, magic markers, pencil, a large piece of "stiff" oaktag or construction paper (piece should be larger than your drawing paper).

DIRECTIONS:

1. Using your pencil or marker, draw symbols associated with Israel on the drawing paper. Symbols can include the Israeli flag, menorah, Jewish star, outline of Israel (see Appendix for patterns). The design can be realistic or abstract. (Even magazine pictures can be used as long as they cover the whole piece of paper.)

2. Color in the entire paper using your magic markers.

3. Fold the oaktag or stiff paper like a fan, starting at one end and folding until you get to the other end.

4. Cut your picture into strips, corresponding to the length and width of the folded oaktag paper.

5. Glue each "picture" strip onto a fold. Use only one side of each fold (either the going "up" or the going "down" of the folds).

6. Draw a second picture on another piece of drawing paper and repeat steps 1 to 5. Your folded paper should now have one picture on the "up" folds and one picture on the "down" folds.

7. When you look at your picture straight on, you will see "multi-images"; when you turn the paper, you will see one picture or the other.

Lag Ba'omer Kite

OBJECTIVES: To study the holiday of Lag Ba'omer.
To make a kite to fly during an outdoor celebration of Lag Ba'omer.

MATERIALS: Several sheets of tissue paper or old wallpaper twenty-by-twenty-four inches, glue, scissors, string, one pipe cleaner.

DIRECTIONS:

1. Cut the paper into a fish body. You need two of the same. Cut long strips for the tail and small shapes for the fins and decorations. Don't forget two eyes (see Figure A).

2. Carefully glue the edge of one fish and place the other on top. Do not glue the mouth. That has to stay open (see Figure B).

3. Make the pipe cleaner into a circle. Insert this into the round mouth of the fish. Glue the paper around the mouth so it is open (see Figure C).

4. Add the eyes, fins, and decorations to both sides. Place the string on each side of the mouth by poking a small hole in the paper. Attach a second long piece to that one. Watch the air puff up your kite! (See Figure D.)

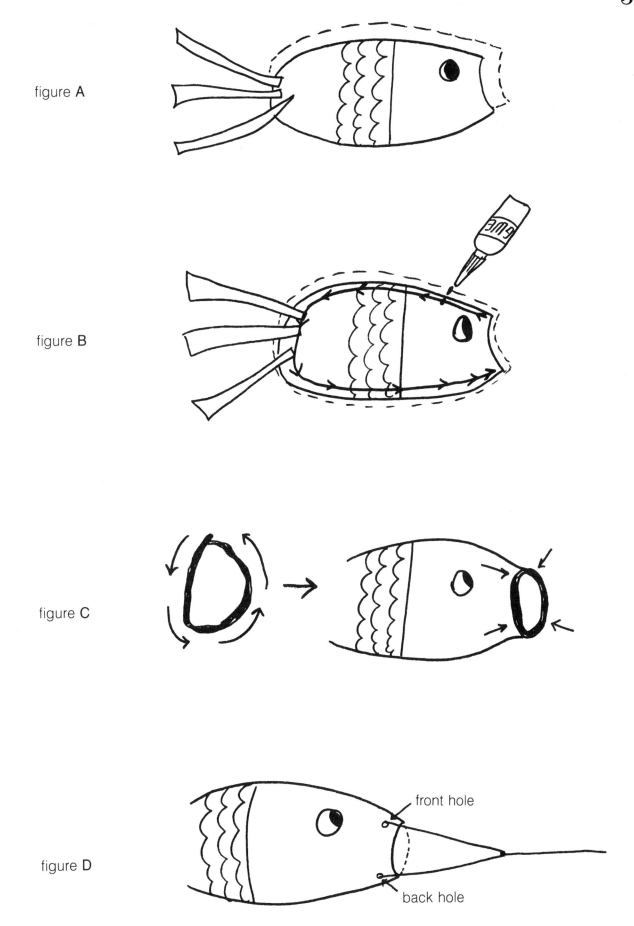

figure A

figure B

figure C

figure D

front hole

back hole

Honoring and helping the aged is and has been a responsibility of all Jews throughout the ages. It is of vital importance to help our children understand the problems of aging. "Experiencing" the effects of aging can add sensitivity to the problems of the aged.

OBJECTIVES: To acquire understanding of the aging process.
To "feel" like an aged person.

DIRECTIONS:

1. *Tactile Impairment.* Cover each fingertip with Scotch tape. Pass around various textured items to experience what a loss of sensitivity to touch is like. Try threading a needle.

2. *Visual Impairment.* Place white cellophane over eyes and try reading a newspaper (Saran Wrap will work as well).

3. *Aged Appearance.* Scrunch your facial muscles. Press Scotch tape at the corners of each wrinkle. Cover face, and tape with face makeup. Add a gray wig. To emphasize each wrinkle, draw brown eyebrow pencil (lightly) under each wrinkle.

4. Photograph each child's made-up face, and put the "aged" photograph on the bulletin board next to the normal pictures.

Bar/Bat Mitzvah Photo Collage

In Exodus 15:2, it states: "This is my God and I will enshrine Him." The Bar/Bat Mitzvah ceremony has included many objects associated with the rituals of Jewish life. Exodus 15:2 has prompted Jews to embellish these ritual items that serve to enshrine God. The Bar/Bat Mitzvah ceremony uses so many of these beautifully created ritual items such as Kiddush cups, candlesticks, prayer books, Torah covers, *yad*s, menorahs, talitim and their bags.

OBJECTIVE: To create a photo collage of symbolic pictures associated with a Bar/Bat Mitzvah ceremony.

MATERIALS: Jewish ritual gift catalog, newspaper or magazines with Jewish content, glue, scissors, oaktag or cardboard nine-by-twelve inches or twelve-by-eighteen inches, clear contact paper (one inch bigger all around than oaktag).

DIRECTIONS:
1. Cut out pictures of ritual items or symbols found in a Bar/Bat Mitzvah ceremony, e.g., Bibles, Hebrew writing, Torah, talit, Kiddush cup, candlesticks, candles, crown, *yad*, prayer book, flowers, certificate.

2. Glue these pictures onto a piece of cardboard, preferably with the pictures overlapping. Cover the entire surface.

3. Peel off the backing of the clear contact paper carefully so as not to crinkle it. Lay the cardboard collage on top of the sticky side of the contact paper. Rub the contact paper over the collage, smoothing out all the bubbles. Fold excess over the edges of the collage.

To make a picture frame from this collage, just cut out a center section of the picture. Tape a photograph in place on the wrong side of the collage. Glue a picture hanger or a paper clip on the back.

34 Marriage Mobile

To create a marriage mobile using the symbols in a marriage ceremony.

MATERIALS: Magazines, drawing paper, magic markers, scissors, glue, colored construction paper, string, fifteen-inch length of bendable wire or a wire hanger, hole-puncher.

DIRECTIONS:

1. Find magazine pictures, or draw pictures that best symbolize the elements of a Jewish marriage.

2. Cut out the pictures and glue them to free-form shapes cut from the colored construction paper.

3. Punch a hole at the top of each shape and place a length of string (vary the lengths of string) through the hole, knotting the end of each.

4. Bend the length of wire to form a circle and secure. (If using a hanger, simply attach the strings to the bottom.) Attach three strings to the circle and draw up to form a tripod. Knot the three strings and form a loop in which to hang the mobile up.

5. Hang the various lengths of string around the circle.

Mezuzah Growth Chart

OBJECTIVES:
To create a Jewish milestone growth chart in the shape of a mezuzah.
To chart a child's "Jewish growth."

MATERIALS:
Piece of felt or burlap five feet long and eight to ten inches wide, trimmings (lace, rickrack, ribbon), thirty-six-inch tape measure, glue, scissors, permanent gold or silver magic markers or paint pens, assorted pieces of felt in several colors, fourteen inches of Velcro, one-inch-thick dowel twelve inches long.

DIRECTIONS:

1. Cut four one-by-five-inch strips from felt pieces. Form loops along the top of the long felt strips. Glue in place. Insert the dowel through the loops so mezuzah can be hung up.

2. Cut out a *shin* from the felt, outline in gold or silver, and glue at the top right-hand corner of the felt mezuzah. (It should be approximately six inches high and three inches wide.)

3. Cut out a felt rectangle four inches long and two inches high. Using the markers, write in the child's name. Glue one seven-inch piece of Velcro to the back of the rectangle and another seven-inch piece to the top of the growth mezuzah. Stick in place.

4. Glue the measuring tape down the middle of the felt mezuzah.

5. Cut out seven two-by-one inch felt rectangles or any Jewish symbol (a Jewish star, Kiddush cup, menorah, etc.). On each one glue an equal length of Velcro. Glue the other half of the Velcro along the bottom of the mezuzah chart. On each felt piece write a different possible milestone that a child might pass—for example, Berit Milah, baby-naming, Consecration, Bar/Bat Mitzvah, Confirmation, marriage, dedication of a new home.

6. Attach these seven Velcro pieces to the matching Velcro backs that are along the bottom of the chart.

7. As the child passes a milestone, glue a Velcro back to the correct height along the measuring tape and attach the proper milestone felt piece.

"Batik" Chupah Cover

The Jewish marriage ceremony takes place under a canopy supported by four poles, a *chupah*. The custom of using a *chupah* originated with the rabbis in the Middle Ages. Custom includes using a floral canopy, your talit, or a canopy of your own making.

OBJECTIVES:
To learn how to make a wax-design batik, using melted crayons.
To create a *chupah*.

MATERIALS:
Crayola crayons (ten to twelve large and peeled crayons of assorted colors), an electric fry pan, ten foil muffin cups, hot water, ten one-half-inch-wide utility brushes, twin bedsheet cut in half, iron, newspapers, magic markers, yellow piece of chalk, cold water dye, bucket.

DIRECTIONS:

1. Heat the electric fry pan on low heat. Add enough water to fill one-third of the pan.

2. Place the foil muffin cups in the heated water. Add to each cup several peeled broken crayons, one color to a cup. Let the crayons melt.

3. With the yellow chalk draw a design on the sheet. Write the word "marriage" or "*chupah*" in the middle. A flower border might be pretty.

4. Dip a brush in the melted crayon color and "paint" it onto the sheet, covering your design. Use a different brush for each color. (The crayon solidifies rapidly once it touches the sheet, so work quickly.)

5. When the sheet has been completely "painted" with the melted crayons, let it dry.

6. Complete your design with the magic marker.

7. Mix the cold water dye according to the instructions. (Rit dye, a hot water dye, is also okay.) Dip the "painted" cloth into the dye for the necessary amount of time. Let dry.

8. Lay the cloth on newspapers. Place a piece of newspaper on top of the cloth. Iron the cloth. The crayon will come off on the top newspaper. When all the crayon has come off, you have a completed "batik" *chupah*.

Though the Bible makes no specific reference to the age of thirteen as the time when a child passes into adulthood, there are strong indications that it isn't a recent innovation. The Talmud (*Mishnah Niddah* 5:6) states that when a vow is made by someone aged thirteen or above, it is a valid vow. In *Ketubot* 50a, a boy of thirteen and a girl of twelve must fast for a full day on Yom Kippur. The clearest statement for choosing age thirteen for the Bar/Bat Mitzvah is found in *Avot* 5:21: "At age thirteen one becomes subject to the Commandments."

OBJECTIVES:

To create a stenciled number-thirteen T-shirt.
To learn how to create a stencil.

MATERIALS:

Cardboard (eighteen-by-twenty-four inches) or heavy oaktag, X-acto knife, white or light-colored T-shirt, can of dark spray enamel paint, lots of newspapers, masking tape, pencil.

DIRECTIONS:

1. In the center of the cardboard, pencil in a six- to seven-inch number thirteen. The numbers should be at least one-half to three-quarters inch wide and two inches apart.

2. Place the cardboard on a thick wad of newspapers. Carefully cut out the numbers using the X-acto knife. Press the knife deeply along the outline of numbers so a sharp edge to the numbers is created. Pop the numbers out. The stencil is now completed.

3. Lay the T-shirt on newspapers (outdoors is preferable, or near an open window). Insert several layers of newspapers inside the T-shirt as well.

4. Tape the number-thirteen stencil to the center front of the T-shirt. Cover whatever part of the T-shirt is showing with several layers of newspapers to prevent it from being sprayed with paint.

5. Spray the number thirteen with the can of paint. Several coats may be needed. Make sure to have adequate ventilation (an open door or window, or being outdoors).

6. Let paint dry completely, then carefully remove all newspapers and the stencil.

7. The stencil can be used repeatedly.

Keriah Wall Hanging

Keriah is the tearing of a garment by a bereaved mourner. The tearing can provide a needed outlet for the pent-up anguish and emotion a mourner feels. At Yom Hashoah we mourn those who died during the period known as the Holocaust.

OBJECTIVES: To express our sense of anguish and feeling of loss through the act of *keriah*, tearing. To create a wall hanging using the tearing of cloth as the medium.

MATERIALS: Fabrics of various colors and designs, eighteen-by-twenty-four-inch piece of dark burlap, four two-by-six-inch strips of felt, glue, a dowel one inch thick and thirty inches long or a broom handle.

DIRECTIONS:

1. Glue the four strips of felt to the top and back of the burlap. They should form four loops in which to place the dowel or broom handle.

2. Cut the fabric into various sizes and shapes. Tear the fabric in parts of each fabric shape. Vary the length and width of each tear.

3. Glue the torn pieces onto the burlap, overlapping some of the pieces.

4. Cut out the word *"keriah"* from the fabric and glue it onto the burlap. You can write it in with magic marker as well.

Marriage Dream Picture in the Style of Marc Chagall

Marc Chagall was a prominent Jewish artist from Russia who lived in France. Many of his paintings are dreamlike in expressing themes found in daily life in the Jewish ghetto.

OBJECTIVE: To create a marriage scene using the dreamlike quality of Marc Chagall.

MATERIALS: Twelve-by-eighteen-inch or eighteen-by-twenty-four-inch white drawing paper, watercolor set, paintbrush, cup of water, small piece of sponge, magic markers, can spray high-gloss varnish or shellac (optional), newspaper.

DIRECTIONS:
1. Lay the drawing paper on the newspaper.

2. Cover the paper with swirls or large dabs of pastel (or soft) colors. A brush or sponge dabbed in the watercolors can be used. Fill the entire paper with these cloudlike puffs of color. Allow to dry. This creates the background.

3. Using the markers, draw a wedding scene over this watercolor background. The drawings need not be filled in. They can remain as outline forms. A bride and groom under a *chupah* can be used. The newly married couple dancing or eating from a piece of wedding cake or any similar scene can be drawn.

4. The finished picture can be sprayed with the glossy shellac to preserve it better and bring out the watercolor background.

A Springtime Wax Paper Mobile

OBJECTIVES:
To create a spring (*aviv*) mobile.
To decorate the home for Passover.

MATERIALS:
Wax paper, tiny scraps of colored tissue paper, thread, a stick, a warm iron, one index card, magic markers, scissors. (Tissue paper can be bought at card, arts-and-crafts, or hobby stores.)

DIRECTIONS:

1. Tear off two pieces of wax paper each a foot long. On one arrange scraps of tissue paper in shapes to look like butterflies or flowers (see Figure A).

2. Carefully place the other piece of wax paper over them, and gently press with a warm iron. (You might need an adult to help with this part.) This will seal the design between the pieces of wax paper.

3. Leaving about a quarter inch around each design, cut out the butterflies and flowers (see Figure B).

4. Tie each of them by threads to a small stick. Write the word "*aviv*" on the index card, and glue the card to the stick. Make each butterfly and flower hang a different length. This mobile will brighten up your seder table (see Figure C).

figure A

figure B

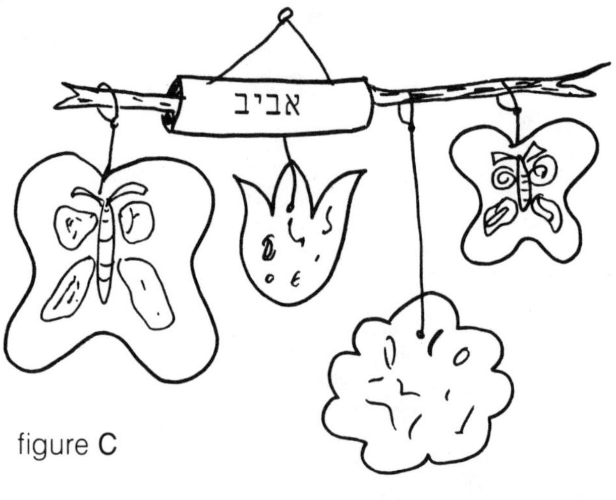

figure C

OBJECTIVES: To create an *afikoman* bag for use at Passover.
To create family "heirlooms" for use at the yearly seder.

MATERIALS: Piece of felt ten-by-twelve inches, twenty-inch piece of ribbon, cord or yarn, trimming (lace, rickrack, cording, etc.), rug yarn for writing word, needle and thread, glue, scissors.

DIRECTIONS:

1. Lay the twenty-inch cord (or ribbon) along the right twelve-inch side (see Figure A). Fold the edge over the ribbon, making sure there is ribbon hanging out of both edges (top and bottom).

2. Using needle and thread, sew down the fold so the ribbon is "trapped" in the pocket (it will be a drawstring to close the bag). Turn it over.

3. Next bring the bottom of the twelve-inch length to the top (see Figure B), and sew the two open edges (the top and left edge). A running stitch or back stitch is fine. Make sure you turn the drawstring edge over before you start to sew. If you don't, then your raw edge will be exposed when the bag is turned inside out.

4. Turn the bag inside out so the raw edge is inside the bag.

5. Spell out the word *"afikoman"* with the glue along the side of the bag. Press the rug yarn along the glue so the yarn spells the word. Let dry.

6. Decorate the bag with bits of trimming.

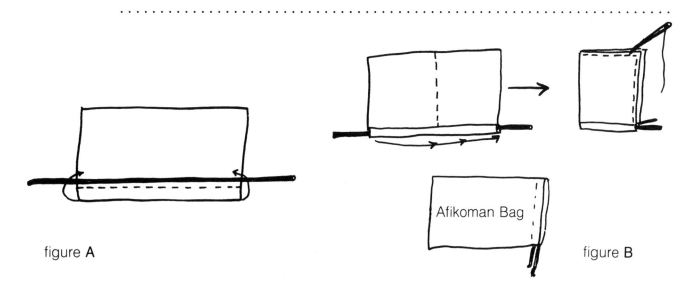

figure A

Afikoman Bag

figure B

A Family Seder Scene

The celebration of Pesach represents the ongoing continuous experience of the Jewish people. Each Jew who participates in the seder service symbolically and vicariously relives the Exodus from Egypt. It is a time for family and friends to gather and celebrate one of the most important events in the history of the Jewish people.

To share personal experiences from our own family's seder.
To create a family seder scene.

Several twelve-by-eighteen-inch pieces of colored construction paper, scissors, glue, magazines, crayons, tinfoil, paper doilies, bits of trim, fabric, and old photographs of your family.

1. You will need a large piece of twelve-by-eighteen-inch construction paper. Fold it so two doors are formed in the front. That is the front of your house (see Figure A).

2. To form a roof, cut a second piece of paper and glue it to the back of the folded house. Cut out and glue on a chimney, too. Now you're ready to decorate it with your family scene at Passover (see Figure B).

3. Using the magazines, drawing paper, crayons, glue, tinfoil, paper doilies, bits of trim, fabric, and old photographs of your family, cut and paste a scene of your family sitting around your Passover table. Your parents can be a photograph or a magazine picture. The food can be drawn or cut from the magazine. The tablecloth can be made from the doilies or the bits of fabric. Put pictures on the walls and anything else that will make it look like your home, like windows on the outside of the flaps (see Figure C).

figure A

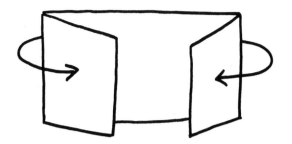

figure B

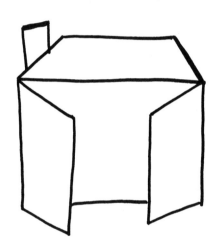

figure C

OBJECTIVES: To create a *charoset* plate to use as part of the Passover seder.

To enjoy the many varieties of *charoset* of *Am Yisrael*.

MATERIALS: One large clear glass plate (it should have no designs or markings), one set permanent magic markers, one piece of white paper cut in the shape of the plate, pencil, three different types of *charoset*, Scotch tape.

DIRECTIONS:

1. Write the word *"charoset"* in the middle of the paper with the pencil. Go over the lines with a dark permanent magic marker. The word should appear backward when the paper is turned over. (This is to help you write the word on the glass plate. Since all the decoration will be on the back of the plate, all words must be written backward on the back so they will appear correct when read on the front of the plate.)

2. Tape the paper on the plate right side up. Turn the plate over. Using the permanent magic markers, trace the word (backward) onto the back of the plate. Divide the plate into three sections either by drawing three wedges, three circles, or three Magen Davids (see Figure A). This will allow you to place the three different types of *charoset* in separate sections on the plate. (See Appendix for *charoset*.)

3. Decorate the edge of the plate with a border of flowers, lines, or a pretty pattern (remember you are still drawing on the back of the plate) using the permanent magic markers. Watercolor markers won't write on glass; only permanent ink markers will.

. . . .

figure **A**

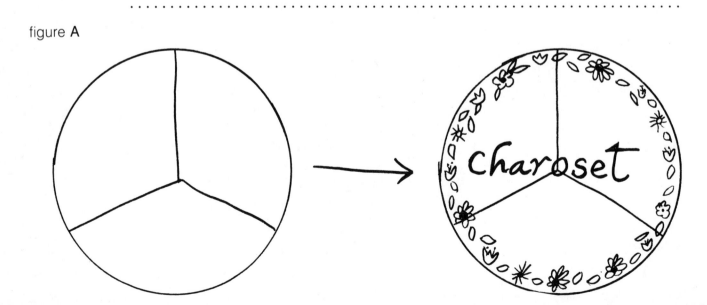

Matzah Magnets

OBJECTIVES: To make magnets from matzah.

To furnish ourselves with a reminder of the Exodus from Egypt.

MATERIALS: Three pieces of matzah, glue, wiggly eyes, bits of felt, fabric or colored paper, yarn, buttons, cut-up pieces of magnetic strip, scissors, spray shellac or clear varnish. (Magnetic strips can be found in any art supply store or in any arts-and-crafts store. If strips cannot be found, small magnetic pieces may be used. These can be found in hardware stores or five-and-tens; wiggly eyes can be purchased in any arts-and-crafts store or five-and-ten.)

DIRECTIONS:

1. Carefully break a sheet of matzah into as many squares or shapes as you can.

2. Using bits of felt, fabric or colored paper, yarn or wiggly eyes, and buttons, create a funny face by gluing these things onto the matzah pieces.

3. Spray shellac or clear varnish onto the front to keep from breaking.

4. Glue a magnet piece to the back of your matzah face when the varnish is dry. Put it onto your refrigerator and . . . it's looking at YOU!

Am Yisrael Jigsaw Puzzle

OBJECTIVES: To create a giant jigsaw puzzle using the maxim of *Am Yisrael*: "Each Jew is responsible for every Jew."
To scatter the puzzle parts and then reassemble them as a group icebreaker.

MATERIALS: A very large piece of poster board, oaktag, cardboard or brown butcher paper, scissors, magic markers, paper bag.

DIRECTIONS:
1. Draw the maxim "Each Jew is responsible for every Jew" in large bold letters in the middle of the poster board, oaktag, cardboard, or brown paper. Color in the letters with the markers. Draw flags from the countries in which Jews are found on the remaining paper or draw pictures or different types of Jews: Yemenite, chasidic, Chinese, Moroccan, Iranian, etc.

2. Cut the picture up into as many pieces as there are people present. Make the shapes interesting and irregular, as a puzzle would be.

3. Put the pieces in a bag. Mix them up. Let each person pull out one. Have the group try to piece the puzzle back together again. Each person should help to reassemble the puzzle.

Clothespin Am Yisrael Doll Display

OBJECTIVES: To create a display of dolls dancing the hora, dressed as the many kinds of Jews in *Am Yisrael*.

To learn how to make dolls from clothespins.

MATERIALS: Bag of wooden clothespins (rounded heads are best for faces), one-half pound self-hardening clay or Play-Doh (see recipe in Appendix), pipe cleaners, yarn, fabric, sequins, magic markers, cotton, felt pieces, buttons, trimming, glue, scissors, one board or piece of heavy cardboard fifteen-by-fifteen inches or larger, aluminum foil to cover the board. (The clothespins, clay, pipe cleaners, and sequins can be purchased in any arts-and-crafts, hobby, or ceramic shop.)

DIRECTIONS:

1. Find pictures of typical folk attire of Jews from around the world: chasidic, Israeli, kibbutznik, Sephardic, Iranian, Indian, etc. (*Encyclopaedia Judaica*).

2. Cover the board with foil.

3. Bend the pipe cleaner around the upper section of the clothespin to form arms.

4. Using markers, sequins, yarn, cotton, and the fabric, create a face and hair on the head of the clothespin.

5. Dress the clothespin according to the folk attire found in pictures. Glue the fabric and trim onto the clothespin for the costume.

6. Form a walnut-sized shape from the clay and place a circle of these forms on the board. Press the clothespin "person" into a clay ball. Let clay dry.

7. Connect all the pipe cleaner hands so the dolls look as if they are dancing the hora.

RESOURCE: Rubens, Alfred. *A History of Jewish Costumes*. New York: Funk and Wagnalls, 1967.

Yotzer, A Prayer of Light and Darkness

OBJECTIVES: To create an interpretive cut-paper picture in which light comes from darkness.
To create black-and-white negative/positive pictures.

MATERIALS: Nine-by-twelve-inch black paper and white paper, scissors, X-acto knife, ruler, white pencil, glue.

DIRECTIONS:

1. On the black paper draw several geometric shapes using the ruler and the white pencil. Try to create several shapes that start small and get bigger and bigger. (See Figure A.)

2. Using the scissors (or the X-acto knife against the edge of the ruler), cut around three of the sides of the rectangular and square shapes and three-quarters of the way around the circular shapes and two sides of the triangular ones.

3. Fold back the cut edges. If there are several shapes within the shape, fold back every other edge. (See Figure B.)

4. Glue the black folded paper onto the white paper.

5. Where there were multiple shapes, glue down every other edge.

6. The result will be light shining through the black folded shapes. A positive/negative picture will be created.

. . . .

figure **A**

figure **B**

white paper

black paper

Purim Puzzle

Are you having a Purim party? Why not mail one piece of this puzzle to each guest. As a mixer, have the guests try to assemble the puzzle. The leading Purim characters are Esther, the queen of Persia; Mordecai, her cousin; Ahasuerus, the king of Persia; Haman, grand vizier to the king; and Vashti, the former queen.

OBJECTIVES:
To make a puzzle using the characters of Purim.
To study the holiday of Purim.

MATERIALS:
Five-by-seven-inch photograph of you in your Purim costume or a piece of drawing paper five-by-seven inches or nine-by-twelve inches, markers, a piece of cardboard the size of the picture, glue, scissors.

DIRECTIONS:
1. Take a photograph of you in your Purim costume. Have the picture enlarged to five-by-seven inches, or draw a picture of one of the Purim characters on the drawing paper. Color it with the markers.

2. Glue the picture onto the piece of cardboard. Let dry thoroughly.

3. Cut the picture into pieces with jagged or free-form shapes.

4. Assemble the pieces.

Shalach Manot Baskets

Mishlo'ach (Shalach) Manot means "the sending of gifts." This custom has its origins in the scroll of Esther. The joyous celebration of Purim has become "an occasion for sending gifts to one another" (Esther 9:19). Among the gifts included are *hamantashen* and money.

OBJECTIVES:

To create *Shalach Manot* (or *Mishlo'ach Manot*) baskets for gift giving.
To fulfill the custom that is part of the Purim celebration.

MATERIALS:

Basket 1—White ten-inch dinner paper plates, two-by-ten-inch strip of oaktag (or plasterboard), magic markers, ribbons, buttons, scissors, stapler, glue.
Basket 2—Plastic strawberry (or cherry tomato) basket, one-half-inch wide ribbon (or whatever width is needed to weave through the holes in the basket), a two-by-ten-inch strip either of stiff ribbon or oaktag for the handle, green tissue paper, stapler.

DIRECTIONS:

Basket 1

1. Fold the paper plate (from the edge to the middle three times) so it looks like a *hamantash*. Staple all three edges so it stays in place (see Figures A, B, and C).

2. Staple the strip onto the folded edges to form a handle.

3. Decorate with the markers, ribbon, and trimming.

4. Fill with sweets and coins.

Basket 2

1. Weave the ribbon in and out of the holes in the strawberry basket. Remember, if one row begins over-under, the next row should be opposite—under-over (see Figure D).

2. Staple the ribbon or oaktag strip to form a handle.

3. Fill the basket with green tissue (one or two sheets). Put sweets and coins inside. Remember to fulfill the custom by giving the gifts to "one another and . . . to the poor" (Esther 9:22).

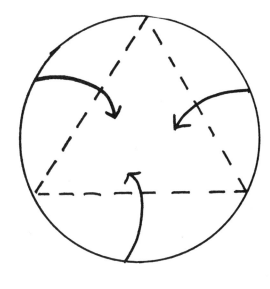

figure A

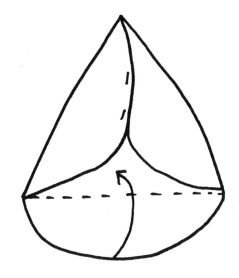

figure B

figure C

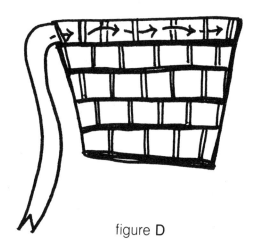

figure D

Purim Stationery—Greetings for Soviet Jews

The holiday of Purim has become the symbolic name for Jewish deliverance. When a community of Jews was saved from a terrible fate, it would celebrate this deliverance by a special Purim for that community. Purim teaches the idea of *Kelal Yisrael* (community of Israel). In times of crisis no Jew is free from the obligation to aid fellow Jews. The Jews in the Soviet Union are in need of support from Jews everywhere. Obtain addresses of refuseniks to whom you can send Purim greetings from the Student Struggle for Soviet Jewry, 200 West 72nd Street, Suites 30–31, New York, N.Y. 10023, or contact your local Soviet Jewry committee.

OBJECTIVES:

To act upon the obligation: "Every Jew is responsible for every other Jew."
To create stationery reflecting the Purim theme.
To write Purim greetings to Soviet Jewish refuseniks.

MATERIALS:

Ink pads (yellow, red, brown, orange) (if pads cannot be found, they can be made by cutting a sponge in four parts, placing in a saucer, and wetting with colored inks), pieces of white paper, envelopes, thick magic markers, gold and silver markers.

DIRECTIONS:

1. Press your fingertip into the ink pad. Put this fingerprint at the top or bottom of the paper. (It will form the face of Queen Esther, King Ahasuerus, Mordecai, or Haman.)

2. You need at least four fingerprints per sheet of paper. Repeat on the front of the envelope in the corner. Let dry thoroughly.

3. Using the markers, create faces on the fingerprints of the Purim characters.

4. Write out (either on top or under the faces): PURIM GREETINGS—BE HAPPY, IT'S ADAR.

5. Write a letter on the stationery and send to a refusenik.

Your Own Purim Megillah (Scroll)

It is a mitzvah to read or hear the scroll of Esther on Purim. Here is an easy way to make your own scroll to read to your family and friends.

OBJECTIVES:

To create your own megillah.

To hear the story of Esther.

MATERIALS:

Toilet paper tube, four pieces of paper four-and-a-half-by-twelve inches taped end to end (see Figure A).

DIRECTIONS:

1. Cut a nine-by-twelve-inch piece of drawing paper in half so it will fit the tube. Roll it up on the tube after you have taped it in place (see Figure B).

2. Color the story of Esther on the drawing paper using pencils or magic markers.

3. Roll up the paper. Make a jacket for your megillah out of fabric or felt by cutting a rectangle (see Figure C) and gluing it around the tube.

4. Decorate the front with glitter or pieces of aluminum foil glued on. Add a foil or paper crown to the top and you have your own *Megillat Esther* (see Figure D).

figure **A**

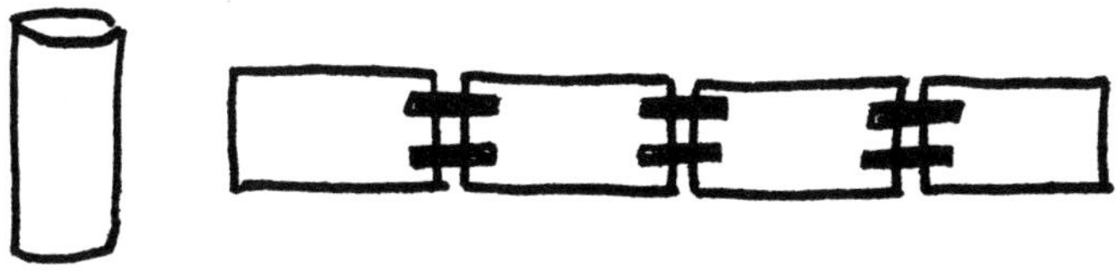

figure **B**

figure **C**

figure **D**

Paper-Strip Purim Mask

OBJECTIVES:

To create paper-strip masks.

To design a mask to be worn at Purim.

MATERIALS:

One large piece of oaktag (or railroad board, as it is sometimes called), six twelve-by-eighteen-inch pieces of colored construction paper, scissors, stapler, glue, feathers, yarn, magic markers.

DIRECTIONS:

1. Cut a strip of oaktag two inches wide by the length necessary to go around your head (see Figure A). Staple the strip so it will form a circle that will fit around your head.

2. Cut three strips one-and-a-half to two inches wide and the length necessary to go across your face at the eyes, nose, and mouth area (see Figure B). Staple the three strips in place. Tie a piece of yarn on either side of the mask to be able to attach it to your face.

3. The basic mask is ready. Now decorate it with the paper, feathers, yarn, and markers.

4. Suggestions for decorations:

Nose—cut a triangle from the oaktag, and fold it down the middle from the point to the side (Figure C).

Hair—use yarn, cotton, or cutout strips of paper (thinner is better) and roll them tightly around a pencil. When you remove them, they will be curly.

figure A

figure B

figure C

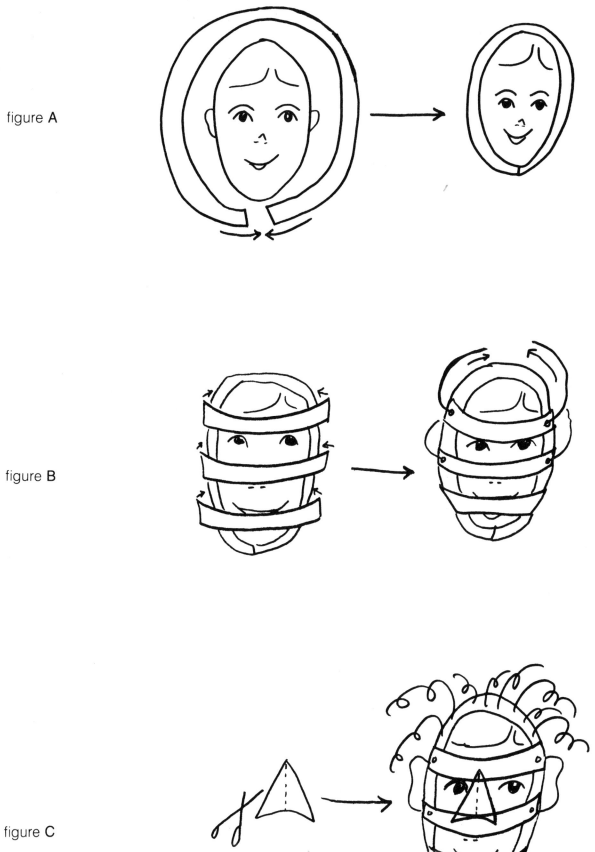

Purim Plaster of Paris Mask

To make a plaster of paris mask in the likeness of one of the Purim characters.
To learn how to use plaster of paris strips.

MATERIALS: Plaster of paris gauze strips (can be bought from an arts-and-crafts store or a medical supply house), Vaseline, ribbon to tie hair away from face, can of warm water, towel, scissors, tempera paints and brushes, yarn, glitter, glue, construction paper, can of spray varnish or polymer.

DIRECTIONS: *Method 1*

1. Coat your face, or that of a friend's, with a thin layer of Vaseline. Tie back the hair from the forehead. Wrap towel around neck.

2. Cut up the strips of dry plaster of paris into pieces approximately two-by-six inches.

3. Dip the strips into the warm water and apply to the face, starting at the forehead, and work your way down to the neck and across to the front of the ears. Go around the eyes and the nostrils. The mouth can be left open or closed. Apply at least three layers of moistened strips.

4. Let dry (about ten to fifteen minutes). Squeeze face while lifting off mask.

5. Cut around edges of the mask to even them out. Paint and decorate the mask with yarn, glitter, and the construction paper. Spray with the varnish. Attach string or yarn to sides to tie to head.

Method 2

1. Blow up a balloon, and lay it on a towel. Coat the front of the balloon with Vaseline and follow steps 2 through 5.

2. To remove the mask, lift off the balloon when dry or pop the balloon.

Shushan Marble Game

The king's palace in Shushan (Susa) was a beautiful place, with rounded doors and a dome roof. King Ahasuerus's palace was typical of those in Persia. Purim is a time for carnivals and parties. This marble game using the palace as the backdrop is a perfect game for Purim.

OBJECTIVE: To create a game for a Purim carnival.

MATERIALS: An empty shoebox, glue, marbles, colored paper, scissors, oaktag, magic markers.

DIRECTIONS:

1. Cut a round dome roof out of the oaktag and glue to the bottom of the box. (Remember, you have to turn the box upside down.)

2. Cut out (from one piece of oaktag) three arched doorways. Glue to the bottom edge.

3. Color in the palace with magic markers or cover it with colored paper. Add rounded windows and you're ready to play. Here is how:

4. Flick the marbles toward the doors. If the marble rolls in, that's worth ten points! Or you can write a different point value above each door. You can use three or four marbles.

5. The person who gets the highest score from rolling in the most marbles through the arched doorways wins.

Rosh Hashanah Card

OBJECTIVES: To create Rosh Hashanah cards.

To use apples, a symbolic food of the holiday, to create the cards.

MATERIALS: An apple cut in half the long way, nine-by-twelve-inch white construction paper, ink pads in several colors, magic markers.

DIRECTIONS:
1. Cut the apple in half (see Figure A).

2. Press half the apple firmly onto the ink pad and then onto the drawing paper. Let dry. (Use different colors.)

3. Fold the paper in half to form a card. The apple print will be on the front and back (see Figure B).

4. Write an appropriate saying in the card. *Leshanah Tovah,* "Happy New Year," is a good saying to write.

. . . .

figure A

figure B

front

back

Leshanah tovah tikatevu vetechatemu—"May you be inscribed and sealed for a good year"— is the customary greeting said to family and friends.

OBJECTIVES:

To create Rosh Hashanah greeting cards.
To create cards from melted crayons.

MATERIALS:

Warming tray and extension cord, aluminum foil (to cover tray top), old crayons, white paper for cards, paper towels (to clean foil of old crayon design), permanent magic markers.

DIRECTIONS:

1. Cover the tray with two layers of foil and then plug in to warm.

2. Peel the crayon and slowly draw a design on top of foil. Crayon will melt as you draw your pattern.

3. Press a whole or folded piece of white paper on top. Design will transfer to the paper or the cloth. Please note: when writing words, you must write them backward if they are to transfer correctly.

4. Wipe the foil clean with the paper towels and start again.

5. When the melted crayon design dries, Rosh Hashanah symbols (apples and honey, rounded chalah, menorah, candles, Kiddush cup) can be drawn over the melted crayons.

6. Write a greeting inside the card.

Rosh Hashanah "Talking" Greeting Card

Leshanah tovah tikatevu vetechatemu—"May you be inscribed and sealed for a good year"— is the Rosh Hashanah greeting expressing the hope that all friends and family will be written and sealed in the Book of Life and granted fulfillment and happiness in the coming year.

OBJECTIVES: To create a Rosh Hashanah card, using the customary greeting for the holiday.
To create a "moving mouth" card.

MATERIALS: Eight-and-a-half-by-eleven-inch construction paper, scissors, magic markers, photographs of your family, glue.

DIRECTIONS:

1. Fold a piece of paper in half the wide way (see Figure A).

2. Cut a three-quarter-inch slip two-and-a-half inches from the left side (see Figure B). Fold down each of the slitted halves.

3. Fold the paper in half again to form a rectangular card. Make sure all the creases of the folds are well pressed down.

4. Open the paper completely. Now fold the paper the long way so the slit is in the middle of the long rectangle facing you (Figure C).

5. Fold the top to the bottom (Figure D) and turn the card on its side. (The folded seam is at the bottom edge.) The front has no slit at the seam, but when the card is opened, the "mouth" inside the card opens and closes to express the Rosh Hashanah greeting. (You may have to adjust the inside folds to make the mouth open and close.)

6. Write the Rosh Hashanah greeting above the opening and closing mouth.

7. On the front glue a photograph of your family (or draw a picture of them with the markers) and write "From all of us—to you. . . ."

61

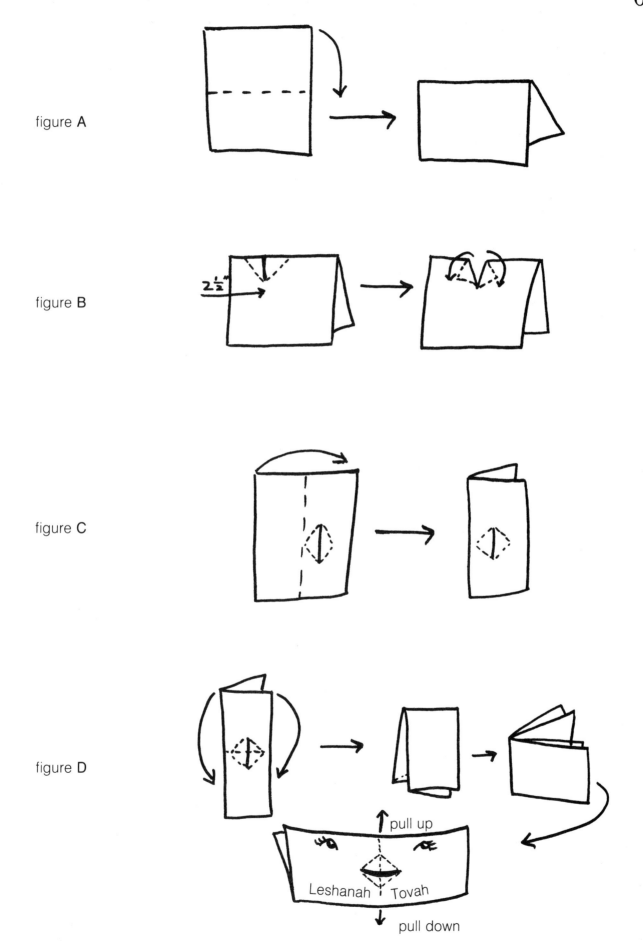

figure A

figure B

figure C

figure D

Dried Apple Face Doll

Apples dipped in honey are part of the Rosh Hashanah tradition. Perhaps the roundness of the apple reminds us of the Jewish cyclical calendar or of the Hebrew word shalom, "peace," whose root also means "complete." The apple with its rounded shape can therefore exemplify the hope for a year of completeness, peace, and unbroken happiness.

OBJECTIVES:

To make dolls, using dried apple faces.
To learn the new skill of apple sculpting.

MATERIALS:

Large apple (pulpy and not too juicy, like a Delicious apple), potato peeler, lemon, nine-inch wire, Lysol spray, fingernail or small pointed scissors, beads, cotton, buttons, fabric, yarn, Elmer's glue, watercolor paint or markers, empty dishwashing liquid bottle, can of clear spray shellac or glass acrylic polymer, pipe cleaner.

DIRECTIONS:

1. Peel apple, leaving a little skin at the top and the bottom. Scoop out two eye hollows with the tip of the peeler (this will leave a raised bump for a nose). Rub apple well with halves of lemon.

2. To hang the apple up to dry, poke the nine-inch wire through the bottom of the core. Push it through the top and bend its end into a hook. Hang the apple for about three weeks away from the sun. On the second of the twenty-one days, spray with Lysol.

3. When apple is dry, cut slit for the eyes and mouth with scissors.

4. Dab glue on beads or buttons, pushing them into the slits you cut for eyes. Paint rosy cheeks with watercolors. After everything dries, spray or brush face with shellac or polymer to give apple a healthy glow.

5. For the bodies fill the empty dishwashing liquid bottle with pebbles to keep them steady. Poke arm holes in sides; thread pipe cleaner arms through the holes. Push the wire necks of the apple head inside bottle, gluing the head in place.

6. To complete the doll, glue on hair of cotton or yarn. Wrap the bottle in fabric scraps, and glue decorations.

Apples and Honey Family Plate

Apples are round and remind us the holiday begins a new cycle of the Jewish calendar and that *rosh* in Hebrew means "head," suggesting roundness. Honey is sweet, symbolizing the sweetness of the New Year we are beginning.

OBJECTIVES:

To create a plate for apples and honey.
To create a family "heirloom" for use each Rosh Hashanah.

MATERIALS:

A round plain glass plate (salad size is fine), a two-to-three-inch round bowl or shot glass, Crazy Glue or Elmer's glue (these can be purchased at any arts-and-crafts or hardware store), *permanent* magic markers or paint sticks (also found in card shops as well as five-and-tens), white piece of paper the size of the salad plate, pencil, and tape.

DIRECTIONS:

1. Write the words "Rosh Hashanah" on the paper circle around the edge (nothing should be drawn in the middle, as the bowl will cover and hide the drawing). You may also include the words "apples and honey" or your family name.

2. Draw pictures of apples, whole or in pieces; bees, beehives, etc., with the pencil on the paper.

3. Tape the drawing paper *upside down* (drawing side facing down against the plate). The pictures will be seen from underneath the plate and act as a guide for the pens.

4. Using the permanent markers or paint pens, trace the drawings on the underside of the plate. (The words will come out backward on the underside of the plate *but* look correct from the top of the plate.) Color in all the designs, filling up most of the plate with color.

5. Using the Crazy Glue (ONLY LET AN *ADULT* use this glue, as it is very-quick-drying and sticky) or the Elmer's glue, glue the smaller bowl or shot glass to the middle of the plate. (If you want to color in this smaller plate, do it before you glue it into the middle of the salad-size plate.) Let dry.

6. Fill the smaller glass with honey and place cut-up pieces of apples around the edge. Use on the first and second nights of Rosh Hashanah holiday season.

A Shabbat Texture Box

Perhaps each member of your family can share one incident that happened in the past week that "felt" like a smooth and warm Shabbat feeling.

To talk about the feelings associated with Shabbat.
To create a texture box that represents the feelings associated with Shabbat.

Shoebox or cigar box, piece of drawing paper (large enough to cover the top of the box), markers, glue, scissors, different pieces of scrap fabric, papers, fur, yarn, cotton, one piece of sandpaper.

1. Glue the paper onto the top of the box.

2. Write the words "Shabbat Textures" in block letters on the top of the box.

3. Cut the fabric to form these two words, using a different fabric for each letter. Glue the fabric (pieces like a collage or a full letter) to the letters.

4. Cut out different pieces of scrap fabric, paper, fur, yarn, and cotton—anything that feels warm and smooth as Shabbat can feel. Each Shabbat another texture can be added.

5. Place the piece of sandpaper in the box. This is to remind us that sometimes our Shabbats are "rough" and not as smooth as we would like them to be.

6. Pass the box around and let your family touch the pieces and see how nice your Shabbat textures feel.

Braided Beeswax Havdalah Candle

OBJECTIVES:

To create a twisted candle for Havdalah.

To create your own Shabbat candle for home services.

MATERIALS:

Wicking cut to the size of the wax piece, scissors, beeswax in sheets.

DIRECTIONS:

Havdalah Candle

1. Cut one sheet in thirds the long way.

2. Cut three pieces of wicking the length of wax.

3. Lay the wick at the bottom edge of the wax (the long side). Roll up like a cigar, entrapping the wick (make sure to leave at least a quarter-inch at the end for burning).

4. After all three pieces have been rolled up to form tubes, lay them down one next to the other. Braid till the end. (Practice braiding first with rope. Pattern is: right over middle piece, then left over middle, etc.)

5. Squeeze the end of the braid to seal candle. Gently squeeze the braid all the way up to close up the spaces for better burning.

Shabbat Candle

1. Cut one sheet in half.

2. Place wick at bottom.

3. Roll up, leaving a quarter-inch of wick at top.

4. Squeeze to shape.

Poland Paper Cuts

Cutting paper to form beautiful designs is an art form popular in Poland. Here's how to cut beautiful paper designs to be used to decorate your Shabbat table.

OBJECTIVES: To learn how to make paper cuts.
To make decorations for our Shabbat table.
To study this popular art form of Poland.

MATERIALS: Eight-and-a-half-by-eleven-inch paper (typing paper is best), scissors, markers.

DIRECTIONS: 1. Cut out a large circle (see Figure A).

2. Fold the circle in half, then in half again (see Figure B). Now you're ready to cut a design.

3. Draw one-quarter of a Star of David in the middle of your folded circle. Fill up the background with wiggly lines and curves (see Figure C).

4. Cut the top edge first in a fancy design, then the inside of the star. Next poke the scissors into the triangular parts of the star and cut them out. Cut between some of the remaining lines. Now open up your circle and look at your paper cut. Try menorahs, flowers, or doves as paper cuts. Or start with a rectangle or a square instead of a circle (see Figure D).

· ·

figure A

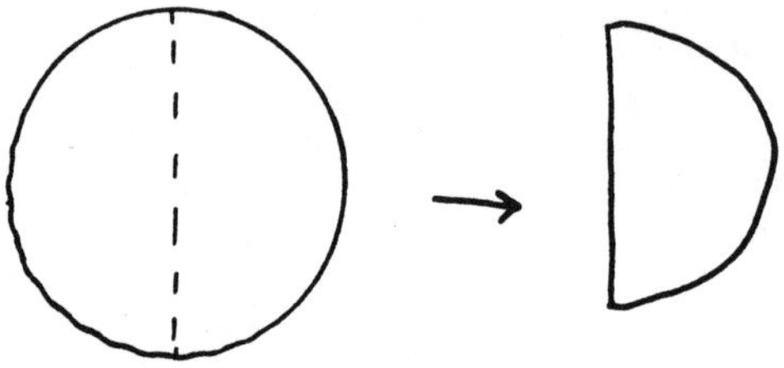

figure B

figure C

figure D

Shabbat Place Mat

OBJECTIVES:
To tie one Shabbat to the next.
To create Shabbat place mats.

MATERIALS:
Eighteen-by-eleven-inch piece of clear contact paper (self-adhesive type), flowers and leaves (if real ones are unavailable, tissue flowers can be used), scissors, colored tissue paper, sequins, colored construction paper.

DIRECTIONS:

1. Place all the materials you will use in front of you. Once you peel the backing off, place all the decorations immediately upon the exposed "sticky" backing.

2. If real flowers are unavailable, cut out flower shapes from the colored tissue paper. Cut out leaf shapes (see Appendix for shape stencils) from the tissue as well.

3. Cut out the word "Shabbat" (English and/or Hebrew) from the colored construction paper. Each letter should be no higher than three inches.

4. Peel off half the backing of the contact paper. Do not peel off all the backing, as it tends to wrinkle (see Figure A).

5. Lay all the flowers, sequins, and the word "Shabbat" on the sticky contact paper. When all the decorations are laid out, peel off the second half of the backing and fold over and onto the decorated half (see Figure B).

Each week make another mat using the previous week's flowers until each member of your family has a mat.

. . . .

figure **A**

figure **B**

Napkin Rings with a Shabbat Twist

OBJECTIVE: To create Shabbat napkin rings.

MATERIALS: Yarn or cord (the thicker the better), wallpaper paste or liquid starch, toilet paper tubes, a cup for paste, wax paper or aluminum foil, glue.

DIRECTIONS:

1. Cut the tubes in half, one half tube for each member in your family.

2. Pour the liquid starch into the cup or mix the wallpaper paste with water until it looks like heavy cream. (Liquid starch can be bought in any grocery store.)

3. Cut the yarn or cord into six-inch pieces (or smaller). Dip one piece into the paste or starch until it is all wet (see Figure A).

4. Shape the wet piece (or pieces of yarn into the letter *shin* or the first initial of the name of someone in your family. Lay it on the wax paper or foil to dry. (You may need several pieces of yarn for each letter. Measure before you wet the yarn so you have the right size and number of pieces.) (See Figure B.)

5. Keep wetting pieces of string and forming either the *bet* or *tav* for the word "Shabbat" or initials of the names of members of your family. Let dry. When hard, lift each letter slowly and glue onto the cardboard tube (see Figure C).

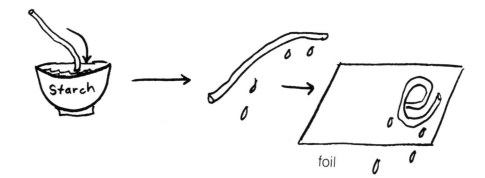

figure A

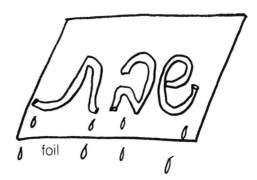

figure B

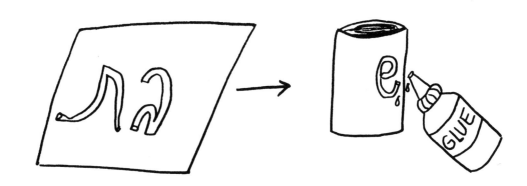

figure C

Eruv for Shalom

An *eruv* is a border put up to allow you to carry any object within an enclosed area on Shabbat. The enclosed space formed by this border is considered a private area within which it is permissible to transport objects. An *eruv* can be used to encircle an individual's private space when he/she wishes to experience shalom.

OBJECTIVES:

To create an *eruv*.
To experience shalom with the creation of an *eruv*.

MATERIALS:

Length of string or wire necessary to encircle a private space (indoors or outdoors), colored construction paper nine-by-twelve inches, colored tissue paper nine-by-twelve inches, markers, scissors, glue, thumbtacks or pushpins, hole-puncher.

DIRECTIONS:

1. Cut out twenty-five to thirty doves from the construction paper (see Appendix for pattern). Glue the wing that faces you onto the body of the dove.

2. Write the word "shalom" on the neck of each dove. Punch a hole in the body.

3. Cut the tissues into flowers (see Appendix for patterns). Place several flower circles on one another and glue each near the middle. Let dry. Punch a hole in the middle.

4. String the doves and the flowers along the full length of the string or wire.

Shabbat in the Style of Shalom of Safed

Shalom of Safed was a prominent "primitive" Israeli artist. His works are easily identifiable by their layered images, bright colors, simplicity of drawing, and colorful borders.

OBJECTIVE: To create a "layered" picture in the style of Shalom of Safed.

MATERIALS: White nine-by-twelve-inch drawing paper, narrow magic markers.

DIRECTIONS:
1. Hold the paper the long way.

2. Draw a half-inch border all around the edges of the paper. Draw six lines evenly divided across and down the paper so there are seven sections as well as the border on the paper.

3. In the border create a floral or geometric pattern, and color it with your markers.

4. Starting at the top section, draw a scene that would be typical for your family on a Sunday. In the second through sixth sections draw typical Monday-through-Friday scenes. In the seventh section draw Shabbat at your home.

Omer Magnets

OBJECTIVES: To learn how to "count the *omer*."
To make *omer* magnets.

MATERIALS: Forty-nine one-by-one-inch white ceramic tiles (these can be bought in any ceramic tile store on one sheet of 144 tiles for under two dollars), a strip of magnetic tape (cut into forty-nine pieces, available in any art supply store or hobby shop), permanent magic markers, one index card.

DIRECTIONS:

1. On each tile write one number from one to forty-nine and the word "day." Use markers.

2. Draw a sheath of barley on each tile with a green or brown marker (see Figure A).

3. Tape a small strip of the magnetic tape to the back of each tile and to the back of the index card.

4. On the front of the index card write the words *"Sefirat Ha'omer."* Color the card.

5. Place this card on your refrigerator. On each night add a magnet with a number day on it. You can form a Star of David with each magnet (see Figure B). On the fiftieth day you celebrate Shavuot.

. . . .

figure **A**

figure **B**

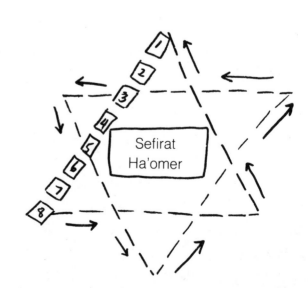

Hammered Copper or Silver Torah Breastplate

OBJECTIVES: To learn a new skill of "hammering" metal.
To make a *choshen*, or breastplate, for a Torah.

MATERIALS: Thirty-six-gauge tooling aluminum or tooling copper eight-and-a-half-by-ten inches (which can be found in any arts-and-crafts store) scissors, newspaper, sixteen-inch piece of heavy string or yarn, hole-puncher, hammer, wide-head nail, newspapers, black cream shoe polish (optional), rag, magic marker.

DIRECTIONS:
1. Make a thick newspaper wad or pillow to rest the metal on.

2. Cut the metal into a breastplate (see Figure A). A regular scissors can be used.

3. On the back of the metal draw a *shin* or a Magen David with the marker.

4. Place the metal (wrong-side up) on the newspaper.

5. The design can be hammered with the nail. Strike the nail with the hammer (gently) along the edge of the design. Tap the nail just hard enough to create an indentation.

6. The metal around the design can be tapped with the head of the hammer to create a curved impression. Cover the whole metal with hammer marks.

7. Turn the metal over and spread a thin coating of dark (black or brown) shoe polish over the breastplate. Let it dry. Rub off the polish with the rag, leaving some polish in the indentations, while rubbing highlights on the raised sections.

8. Punch holes in each corner of the breastplate. Attach cord.

. . . .

figure **A**

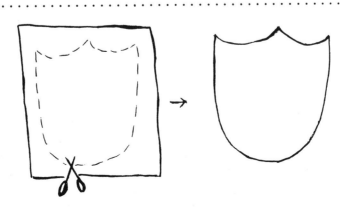

Stretched Paper Decorations for the Sukah

OBJECTIVE: To create stretchy paper.

MATERIALS: Eight-and-a-half-by-eleven-inch paper (typing paper is great), scissors, and lots of patience.

DIRECTIONS:
1. Fold the paper in half the long way. Fold it again so it forms a long column (see Figures A and B).

2. Cut a half-inch fringe along the bottom almost to the top of the paper but not quite (see Figure C).

3. Turn the paper over so you can cut in between the cuts, again almost to the top but not quite (see Figure D).

4. Unfold the paper all the way (see Figure E).

5. Now stretch the paper.

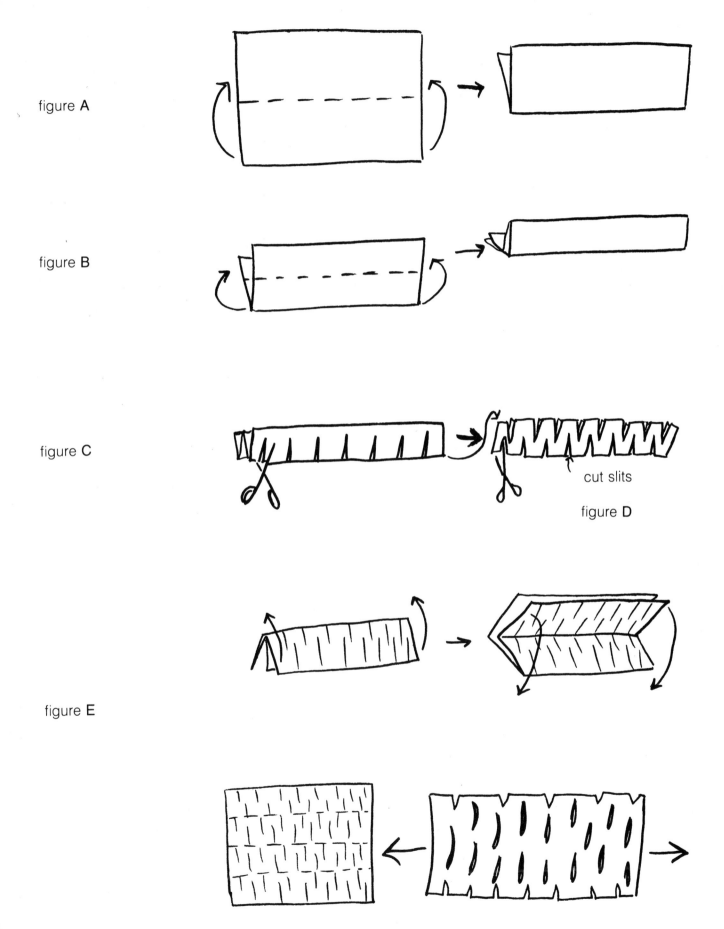

figure A

figure B

figure C

cut slits

figure D

figure E

Ushpizin (Guests) for the Sukah

There is a custom of inviting *ushpizin*—symbolic guests—each day into the sukah. The Kabbalists from Safed popularized this custom. Sephardic Jews set aside an ornate chair for the honored guests and recite: "This is the chair of the *ushpizin*."

OBJECTIVES:

To create a guest list of favorite heroes/heroines.
To make life-size *ushpizin* for the sukah.

MATERIALS:

Brown paper on a roll (the height of a person) or butcher paper, colored construction paper, scissors, yarn, wiggly eyes, buttons, trim, fabric pieces, glue, magic markers.

DIRECTIONS:

1. Cut a piece of brown paper the length of a person. Lay a person down on the rolled-out paper. Trace the person's outline on the paper with the marker. Cut out the body and tape to a wall.

2. Decorate the cut-out figure to look like the *ushpizin* you have invited into your sukah. Use the yarn for hair; paper and fabric for clothing; buttons or wiggly eyes for the face.

3. Write the guest's name on a piece of paper and glue to the hand. A short biography can be included.

4. You can actually put these life-size *ushpizin* in your sukah or around your classroom or home as decorations.

Pointillist Still Life in the Style of Georges Seurat

Fruits from the fall harvests such as apples, pears, cranberries, pumpkins, and gourds are often used to decorate a sukah. Georges Seurat used points of color to capture the impression of fruit images. He is known as a French Impressionist painter.

OBJECTIVES: To create a picture using the pointillist style of Georges Seurat.
To create a still life, using the fruits of the fall harvest.

MATERIALS: Q-Tips, watercolor set, white drawing paper (any size), still life of apples, pumpkins, grapes, etc. (any fall fruits).

DIRECTIONS:

1. Set up a still-life display of various fall fruits.

2. Using Q-Tips moistened slightly in water and then rubbed (or dipped) into watercolor paints, outline in dots or points (created by the top of the Q-Tip) the shape of the fruits in the still life.

3. Fill in the outline with dots of colors (close to natural fruit colors) until the whole paper, including the background (if you wish), is filled. Keep changing Q-Tips as needed.

4. If the background is filled in with dots of color, make sure a contrasting color like black, white, or blue is used.

5. Place both the fruits from your still life and your pointillist picture in your sukah.

Replica of a Wooden European Synagogue

Many synagogues throughout Europe were made of wood. Data can be solicited from the Jewish Museum in New York City, the Skirball Museum at HUC-JIR in Los Angeles, or the Museum of the Diaspora in Tel Aviv as to what these wooden synagogues looked like.

OBJECTIVES:

To replicate a wooden synagogue from Europe.
To do research on gathering data on wooden synagogues.

MATERIALS:

Two sheets eight-and-a-half-by-eleven inches balsa wood, box of one thousand wooden ice cream sticks, glue, tempera paint, brush, wooden or cardboard eight-and-a-half-by-eleven-inch board, newspaper to work on, X-acto knife.

DIRECTIONS:

1. Place the board on the newspaper.

2. Placing the sticks end to end, form three sides of a rectangle around the board. Glue layer after layer of sticks until the structure reaches five inches high. This will give you the basic foundation of the synagogue. Don't forget to leave the short front side empty for the front door section.

3. Using a photograph of one of the synagogues, continue working up the sticks to duplicate the structure in the picture.

4. The roof and the doors can be cut from the pieces of balsa wood and glued into place.

5. When the structure is dry, paint with the tempera colors.

Ner Tamid of Punched Metal

Above the ark (*Aron Hakodesh*) is located the *Ner Tamid*—the Eternal Light—recalling the Eternal Light in the Temple as found in the Book of Exodus 27:20–21. The light never goes out.

OBJECTIVE: To make a *Ner Tamid* from a metal can.

MATERIALS: A metal can (size of a can of coffee), a nail and a hammer, a light bulb (sixty watts and under) set up on a wire, newspaper, towel, magic marker.

DIRECTIONS:

1. Remove the top of the can. Fill the can with water and place in freezer overnight.

2. Place can on towel on its side (only if water is frozen solid). Newspapers should be under the towel to soak up drips as the ice melts.

3. Draw line symbols of Judaism around the can: stars, menorahs, etc. (see Figure A).

4. The tin is easily pierced with a hammer and nail when the water is frozen. Hammer evenly spaced nail holes through the lines of the pattern.

5. Remove the bottom of the can after all the holes have been punched.

6. Place the bulb setup through the can and hang above your *Aron Hakodesh*.

If your class or home has an *Aron Hakodesh*, this makes a wonderful addition to the parts of a synagogue.

. . . .

figure **A**

OBJECTIVES: To create a memorial book using selections from the Book of Lamentations.

To write and illustrate poems that illustrate the word "destruction."

To put to paper the feelings aroused by the word "destruction."

MATERIALS: Sheets of eight-and-a-half-by-eleven-inch paper, magic markers, one piece of oaktag or cardboard nine-by-twelve inches, stapler.

DIRECTIONS:

1. Fold the sheets of paper in half. Staple them along the fold.

2. Fold the cardboard in half. Place the sheets of paper on top of the folded cardboard. Staple along the seam.

3. Choose a selection from the Book of Lamentations to put on the cover of this memorial book. Examples:

   "All our enemies have opened their mouth wide against us" (3:46).

   "He hath caused the arrows of His quiver to enter into my reins" (3:13).

   "Judah is gone into exile because of affliction and because of great servitude" (1:3).

4. Using fancy writing or calligraphy, draw your quote on the cover of the memorial book.

5. Create poems, haiku, or essays about the word "destruction" on each of the pages in the memorial book.

6. Illustrate each page with appropriate symbols and drawings for the written material.

Rebuilt Western Wall

OBJECTIVE: To construct a model of the Western Wall, *Kotel Hama'aravi.*

MATERIALS: Sugar cubes (one box), white craft glue, tempera paint in light golden tan or beige (mix brown, yellow, and white paint), green pipe cleaners, brush, one block of wood, piece of heavy cardboard or top of a carton, one index card, magic marker.

DIRECTIONS:
1. Glue the sugar cubes together to look like a brick wall.

2. Paint the sugar cube "Western Wall." Let dry.

3. Glue pieces of green pipe cleaners into the cracks of the wall to represent the caper plants that grow on the Western Wall.

4. Glue the wall to the wood block, cardboard, or carton.

5. Write *"Hakotel"* on the index card and place on the sugar cube wall.

82 Tree Treats Collage for Tu Bishvat

OBJECTIVES: To learn about the treats trees give to us all.
To celebrate the holiday of Tu Bishvat.

MATERIALS: One large piece of drawing paper twelve-by-eighteen inches, magic markers, old magazines, scissors, glue.

DIRECTIONS:

1. Holding the paper the long way, place your hand flat on it. Trace the outline of your hand and arm on the paper with the markers (black or brown) (see Figure A).

2. Color the outline of your hand and arm so it looks like a tree. Write the words "Tree Treats" down the sides of the paper (see Figure B).

3. From the old magazines cut out pictures showing any product from a tree: fruits, furniture, nuts, paper, books, pencils. Glue the pictures on the branches of the tree as if they were leaves. Hang them up and see if your family, friends, and classmates can identify all the "Tree Treats."

. . . .

TREE TREATS

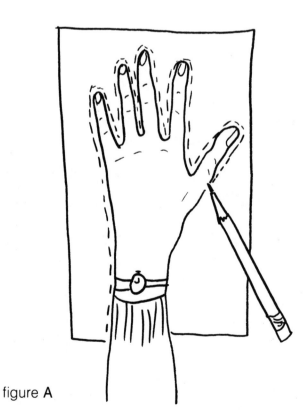

figure A

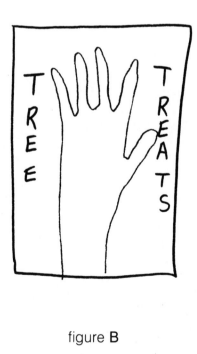

figure B

Since almond trees are in bloom in February in Israel, why not add cotton balls and pink flowers to your tree.

OBJECTIVES: To create straw-blown trees with cotton "almond" blossoms (almond trees are the first trees to flower in Israel).
To study the holiday of Tu Bishvat.

MATERIALS: A nine-by-twelve-inch piece of smooth paper (watercolor paper, butcher paper, or wax-coated paper), brown ink or watered-down brown tempera paint, straw, crayons or markers, cotton balls, glue.

DIRECTIONS:
1. Take a piece of butcher paper (nine-by-twelve inches) or any smooth piece of nine-by-twelve-inch paper.

2. Add a drop or two of ink at the bottom of the paper. Brown ink is best but brown tempera paint, watered down, is good too.

3. Next get a straw and start blowing the ink toward the top of the paper. Move the paper around so a trunklike shape is created (see Figure A).

4. Add leaves with crayons, colored pencils, or magic markers (see Figure B).

. . . .

figure A

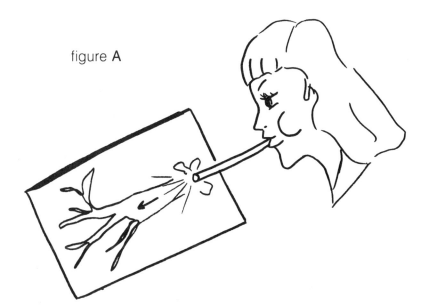

figure B

Tree Branch Weaving for Tu Bishvat

OBJECTIVES:
To study the importance of trees.
To learn how to weave a tree branch.

MATERIALS:
Ball of self-hardening clay, a small tree branch with several outstretched twigs, yarn, magazine, colored construction paper, scissors, glue.

DIRECTIONS:

1. Push the bottom of the branch (a small branch is okay) into the ball of clay (see Figure A).

2. Wind an arm's length of yarn around the branch. Do this with three pieces of yarn (see Figure B).

3. Now start to "weave" a new piece of yarn over and under the rows of yarn on the branch. If you weave over a thread on row one, go under the thread on the next row. Keep going over and under the yarns until all the rows of yarn on the branch are filled (see Figure C).

4. Cut out pictures of products that come from or are made from trees. Glue them onto the colored paper. Cut out free-form shapes. Keep them small—around two inches wide and two inches long.

5. Glue each picture to the woven yarn.

. . . .

figure **A**

figure **B**

figure **C**

Tu Bishvat Planter with Parsley

OBJECTIVES:
To study the value trees have to us in our life.
To make a planter from wooden sticks.
To plant parsley for a Passover harvesting.

MATERIALS:
Packet of parsley seeds, planting soil, piece of aluminum foil, ice cream sticks, glue, plastic bag, spray paint (optional), one-half cup pebbles or small rocks.

DIRECTIONS:
1. Form a square with the ice cream sticks. Glue at corners (see Figure A).

2. Lay a row of sticks end to end across the square, gluing as you go. (This is the bottom of the planter.)

3. Form another square on top of the planter bottom, gluing the corners as you lay down each of the four sticks.

4. Keep building up the sides until your planter is at least six to eight inches high. Let dry. (It is optional to spray-paint the planter.)

5. Line the planter with the aluminum foil. Put a layer of pebbles at the bottom for better drainage.

6. Fill the planter with soil until one inch from the top.

7. Make several pencil holes in the soil. Sprinkle several parsley seeds into the hole. Cover with soil.

8. Water the planting.

9. Cover the planter with a plastic bag that has been closed. (This will give the seedlings moister surroundings in which to begin to sprout.) Leave the bag on (but keep opening to water) until seedlings appear.

If planted during Tu Bishvat, the parsley can be harvested by Passover and used during the seder, thus connecting one holiday to another.

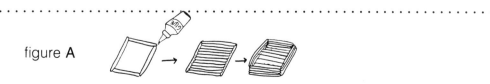

figure A

Tzedakah Support Stabile

OBJECTIVES: To construct a *tzedakah* support stabile.

To symbolize the concept of *tzedakah* as the support of another human.

MATERIALS: Thin rubber gloves, plaster of paris, nine-by-twelve-inch board, a miniature Torah, a plastic replica of a person, glue, hammer and nails, can of spray paint in silver or gold.

DIRECTIONS:

1. Mix the plaster of paris according to directions. Fill the gloves one at a time. Hold them until the plaster begins to harden. Quickly shape each hand as if it were holding an object. When the plaster is hard and the shape is set, nail the hands onto the board.

2. Spray the hands and the board either gold or silver.

3. Glue the miniature Torah somewhat opened onto the capped hands. Let dry.

4. Glue the miniature figure on top of the Torah. Let dry.

Shalom (Peace) Plaster Balloons

The concept of shalom is not only of peace but of wholeness or completeness.

OBJECTIVES: To create shalom plaster balloons.
To have fun making shalom decorations.

MATERIALS: Ball of cotton string, plaster of paris, bowl or can of warm water, balloons, hanger, cans of spray enamel in pastel colors.

DIRECTIONS:

1. Blow up balloons. Tie a string around each neck and hang from a hanger. Hang the hanger on a nail or hook so both your hands are free. Place newspaper under balloons.

2. Prepare the plaster of paris according to directions. Do not make more than one can (the size of coffee) at a time, as the plaster dries quickly.

3. Cut several long lengths of string (around twenty-four inches). Dip in plaster mixture, coating each string and then wrapping it around the balloon. Keep wrapping strings soaked with plaster around the balloon until it is covered. Do each balloon the same way. Let dry completely.

4. Break the balloon once plaster is dry.

5. Spray the balloons. Let dry.

6. To make a shalom mobile, hang several pastel balloons on a hanger and write the words "shalom," "peace," "completeness."

Chesed (Lovingkindness) Woven Collage

OBJECTIVES: To "weave" *chesed* (lovingkindness) through our lives.
To create a collage of woven magazine pictures.

MATERIALS: Nine-by-twelve-inch construction paper, scissors, magazines, glue, magic marker, eighteen-by-twenty-four-inch piece of drawing paper, tape.

DIRECTIONS:

1. Cut slits one-half to one inch apart across a nine-by-twelve-inch piece of colored construction paper. On another piece cut the slits down the paper (see Figure A). Make sure to leave a one-inch border all around the paper.

2. Cut out varying widths (one-quarter to one inch) of strips the width of the colored paper. Cut out several strips of one color. Write the word *"chesed"* all over these strips.

3. Start to weave the strips through the slitted paper (see Figure B). Starting at one edge, weave the strip in an under-over-under-over pattern all across the paper, then glue the end in place. On the second row weave in an opposite pattern, beginning with an over-under-over-under pattern. Make sure to weave one-inch *chesed* strip through the design.

4. Weave five to six different papers, making sure a *chesed* strip is woven throughout each one.

5. Tape the backs of each woven paper to firmly secure the strips.

6. Cut out free-form or geometric shapes from the woven papers. Put aside.

7. Cut out magazine pictures symbolic of all the things that represent your interests: family, hobbies, personality, etc.

8. Glue both the woven shapes and the magazine pictures onto the eighteen-by-twenty-four-inch paper, overlapping edges of shapes and pictures.

. . . .

figure **A**  figure **B**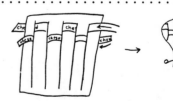

OBJECTIVES: To perform an act of *chesed* (lovingkindness).

To make an oversize bib for an adult in need of one (at a nursing home, hospital, etc.).

MATERIALS: Long vinyl tablecloth with flannel backing, scissors, ribbons for tying, permanent magic markers, needle and thread, trim, glue.

DIRECTIONS:

1. Cut out as many bibs as you can from the tablecloth. They should be at least twelve inches wide and twelve inches long. Once cut, these squares can be rounded off at the bottom and neck to look and fit better.

2. Sew a piece of ribbon twelve inches long to each neck edge (see Figure A). This can be glued as well.

3. Draw faces or designs on the front with the permanent markers. These markers can be purchased in art supply or stationery stores and come in all colors as well as gold and silver.

4. Optional: you can glue trimming to the bib.

5. Wrap the bibs in pretty paper and deliver them to the adults in homes or hospitals as your act of *chesed* (lovingkindness).

. . . .

figure A

Sefer (Book) Savers:
Two Bookmarks to Make and Give

OBJECTIVES:

To learn the Hebrew word for book (*sefer*).
To make two kinds of bookmarks.

MATERIALS:

Clear contact paper, bits of colored tissue paper, sequins, tinfoil shapes, glitter, real flowers and leaves, permanent magic markers, wooden spring clothespin, one inch circle cut from oaktag.

DIRECTIONS:

First Bookmark

Cut a piece of clear contact paper in a strip about four-by-eleven inches (it is sold in wallpaper or hardware stores). Slowly peel the backing off the contact paper. Then decorate half the contact paper with flowers, leaves, glitter, bits of colored paper, tinfoil shapes, tiny buttons. Fold the empty half of contact paper onto the decorated part, forming a sandwich of clear contact paper with decorations in the middle. Write "Sefer Saver" on the front (see Figure A).

Second Bookmark

Using watercolor or magic markers, paint decorations on the sides of a wooden clothespin. From a piece of drawing paper cut a circle the size of a quarter. Draw a smiling face on it and glue it on one leg on the open end of the clothespin. Write "Sefer Saver" down the front of the clothespin (see Figures B and C).

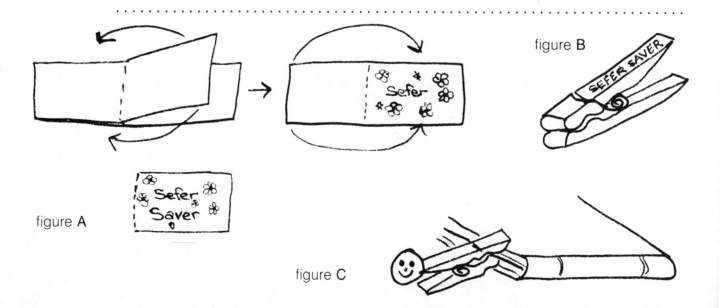

figure B

figure A

figure C

Talmud Torah Keneged Kulam
Representational Stabile

Using the phrase *Talmud Torah Keneged Kulam*, usually translated as "The study of Torah is equal to them [mitzvot] all," a stabile (standing mobile) can be made in which a concept and/or definition implied in each word is represented.

Talmud—Student concentrating on a page of text (bent balsa wood)

Torah—Divine book (glitter tossed on glued or sprayed wood, representing divine sparks)

Keneged—The ability of study to make a lasting impression (hands pushed into plaster)

Kulam—"All else" (collage of shapes, colors, and textures)

OBJECTIVES:
To create a sculpture or stabile that represents *Talmud Torah Keneged Kulam*.
To explore multimedia.

MATERIALS:
Twelve-by-twelve-inch piece of thin balsa wood, stapler, glue, piece of wood for stand twenty-four-by-eighteen inches, can of spray paint (white or silver), shoebox, plaster of paris, glitter, magazine, bits of fabric, sandpaper, corrugated paper, tissue paper, nine-by-twelve-inch oaktag, masking tape, scissors.

DIRECTIONS:

1. Soak the balsa wood until thoroughly wet. Bend the wood around a beach, soccer, rubber, or basketball. Tape the ends to the ball so it will stay on the ball until the wood dries. Remove when dry. Spray wood on both sides with paint. Let dry.

2. Spray the wood rectangle with the paint on the top and sides. Let dry.

3. Staple bent balsa wood to the piece of wood so balsa wood is bent across the base.

4. Glue the top of the base or spray with paint again. Scatter glitter across the top. Dust off excess glitter.

5. Mix the plaster of paris according to directions. Pour the creamlike mixture into the shoebox. Push your hands into the drying plaster of paris while it is still soft. Wash off your hands and let plaster dry. Peel the shoebox away from the plaster when it is completely hardened. Glue the plaster onto the wooden base beneath the bent piece of balsa wood.

6. Create a collage of shapes cut from the fabric, sandpaper, magazine, and papers. Glue the overlapping pieces onto the oaktag. Attach the collage (when dry) to one of the sides of the wooden base (staple or glue). View the melding of the many materials used in making a representational collage of the Hebrew phrase *Talmud Torah Keneged Kulam*.

Mizrach Means East

A uniquely Jewish wall decoration, perfect for any room in the house as a special marker for the eastern wall, which is known as a *Mizrach*. Facing eastward reminds the Jews in the Diaspora where the Temple once stood.

OBJECTIVES:

To learn what a *Mizrach* is.
To create three different kinds of *Mizrachim*.

MATERIALS:

Heavy-duty foil, colored construction paper, nine-by-twelve-inch colored oaktag, permanent magic markers, glue, yarn, scissors, toothpicks, watercolor paints and brush, spray can of shellac.

DIRECTIONS:

Foil Mizrach

Tear a piece of heavy-duty foil eight-and-a-half-by-eleven inches and fold in half (see Figure A). Smooth the foil out so it lies flat. Glue the foil to a bigger piece of colored paper. Use a pencil to write the word *"Mizrach"* in Hebrew or English into the foil. Color the foil with permanent magic markers (see Figure B).

Yarn Mizrach

Draw the word *"Mizrach"* in bubble letters on a piece of cardboard or oaktag (nine-by-twelve inches). Fill in one letter at a time with glue. Then fill in the letter with a piece of yarn (see Figure C). When one letter is done, go on to the next until all the letters are finished. Then fill in the background with another color yarn or magic markers (see Figure D).

Toothpick Mizrach

Draw the word *"Mizrach"* in bubble letters as you did in the yarn *Mizrach* on a piece of oaktag nine-by-twelve inches (see Figure E). Fill in one letter at a time with glue, and place toothpicks so they fill up the whole letter. Cut the toothpicks so they fit the little spaces of each letter (see Figure F). When all the letters are done, use paint or magic markers to color them in. You can spray them with shellac or hair spray to make them shiny (see Figure F).

figure A

figure B

figure C

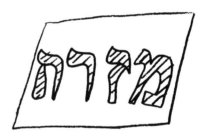

figure D

figure E

figure F

Tzedakah Coin Can (Pushka)

OBJECTIVES: To make a personal *tzedakah* can (*pushka*).
To collect money to be given to those in need.

MATERIALS: Empty can of scouring cleanser, construction paper, glue, gold or silver point pen, coin catalog, rolled coin papers, brush, jar of glossy acrylic polymer, nail and hammer, scissors.

DIRECTIONS:

1. Line up nail holes in the middle of the top of the can so they form a slit for the coins to enter. Use a quarter for the length needed for a slit.

2. Cut the construction paper so it forms a jacket over the can. Glue in place.

3. Cut out pictures of coins and paper money from the coin catalogs and glue onto construction paper, overlapping pictures. Cut the paper coin rolls in half and glue them onto the construction paper. Cover completely.

4. When glue on pictures is dry, write the word "*tzedakah*" on the can in gold or silver. When paint dries, brush several coats of glossy polymer over the collage of coins. Let dry.

A Microtopography Picture

Jews have often developed unique art forms to decorate their precious books. A long time ago Jews decorated their siddurim and haggadot with tiny words creating beautiful shapes, designs, and realistic forms. These tiny words were often descriptive of what they formed. Sometimes they were prayers or stories that formed images of what they referred to.

OBJECTIVES:

To make a microtopography picture.
To learn about and appreciate a unique Jewish art form.

MATERIALS:

Drawing paper twelve-by-eighteen inches or larger, narrow-pointed magic markers, pencils, frame for picture.

DIRECTIONS:

1. Draw a thin pencil line design as a guide for the tiny words. Pictures of Jewish symbols, a Shabbat scene, a Passover scene, the outline of the city of Jerusalem, or the word "shalom" are wonderful ideas for the picture.

2. Using tiny words representing the area drawn or the word itself, such as "shalom," create an overall design with magic markers. It can be just an outline or a completely filled-in design.

3. Mount and frame.

. . . .

SHOFAR

Coin Purse/Comb Case for around the Waist

Many aged people use canes or walkers and therefore find it difficult to hold a purse in their hands. A gift of a purse that can hang from a belt and thereby free the hands would be most appreciated by an older person. It is an act of *chesed*, lovingkindness, to give such a gift.

OBJECTIVES:

To make useful gifts for the aged.

To do an act of *chesed* (lovingkindness).

MATERIALS:

Heavy felt rectangle six inches wide by eleven inches long, yarn, yarn needle, one-inch piece of Velcro, trimming (lace, rickrack), glue, scissors, assorted pieces of felt in various colors, scraps of fabric.

DIRECTIONS:

1. Fold the rectangular piece of felt so it forms a purse (see Figure A). Bring the bottom halfway up and the top piece over the fold.

2. Sew the sides of the purse using either a back stitch, a running stitch, or a blanket stitch (see Figure B).

3. Cut out two strips two inches wide and three inches long. Sew the strips to the back of the purse so they form two loops (see Figure C). A belt can go into these loops so the purse can hang from the wearer's waist.

4. Separate the Velcro. Sew one piece to the folded section and one piece on the inside of the flap. When the flap is folded down onto the pocket section, it will close the purse.

5. Glue on trim to decorate the purse.

To make a comb case, follow directions for the purse but change the dimensions of the felt piece to fourteen inches long by three inches wide.

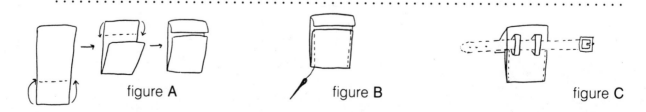

figure A   figure B   figure C

Decorated Tzedakah Shopping Bag for Food Collection

OBJECTIVES: To collect food for those in need.

To create a shopping bag with the word *"tzedek."*

MATERIALS: One plain brown or white shopping bag, magic markers, gold or silver paint pen, labels from food cans, glue.

DIRECTIONS:

1. Write the word *"tzedek"*—righteousness, justice—on the front and back of the bag with the gold and/or silver paint pen. The Hebrew and English should be used.

2. Decorate the bag with drawn pictures or a collage of labels from food cans glued onto the bag.

3. Use the bags for collecting food for a local shelter for the homeless, soup kitchen, or local agency that distributes food to the needy and aged.

A Lechayim Living Picture

OBJECTIVES: To learn the word *"Lechayim."*

To create a "living" picture, using parsley seeds as our art media.

To grow parsley greens for use in our seder.

MATERIALS: Potting soil, a shoebox, tinfoil, parsley seeds, an orange stick or pencil, plastic wrap.

DIRECTIONS:

1. Line the shoebox with the tinfoil.

2. Fill the box with the potting soil until one inch from the top of the shoebox.

3. Using the orange stick or the pencil, poke holes in the soil so they form the word *"Lechayim."*

4. Place several parsley seeds into each of the holes that form the word *"Lechayim."* Cover the holes with a thin layer of soil. Water lightly.

5. Place a layer of plastic wrap over the top of the box. Put in a sunny location.

6. Harvest the parsley in about six weeks. Plan your planting accordingly, so it will be available for your seder at Passover.

Yom Hashoah Magazine Collage

OBJECTIVES: To express nonverbally the many feelings associated with Yom Hashoah.
To create a collage from pictures that express these diverse feelings.

MATERIALS: Eighteen-by-twenty-four-inch drawing/construction paper, glue, scissors, magazines, magic marker.

DIRECTIONS:

1. Cut out pictures that express both feelings of sadness and anger as well as pride and hope.

2. Glue these pictures onto the paper, either interspersing them or clearly separating the two groups of feeling pictures.

3. Using the marker, write the words expressing these feelings in bold letters on the paper.

Kristallnacht, "Night of Broken Glass," Collage of Broken Glass

November 9, 1988 marked the fiftieth anniversary of Hitler's approved "Night of Broken Glass." Nazis throughout Germany ignited fires and broke glass from the windows of synagogues and homes. On that night of shattered glass, over seven thousand businesses were destroyed, nearly one hundred Jews were murdered, and about thirty thousand Jewish men were arrested.

OBJECTIVES:

To create a collage using broken glass as the medium.

To study the "Night of Broken Glass."

To create a picture expressing the feelings associated with that event.

MATERIALS:

Broken car windshield glass (go to any car replacement glass store and ask for their broken windshield glass. It is very safe, as there are *no* sharp edges. It is laminated and tempered and breaks into rounded edges, not sharp ones), glue, nine-by-twelve-inch piece of oaktag, permanent magic markers, pencil.

DIRECTIONS:

1. Draw a picture symbolizing the terror and fear of that night of November 9, 1938, in Germany. One example could be a star being consumed by flames or a synagogue in flames. If a symbolic picture is wanted, just draw sharp, jagged shapes connecting and overlapping.

2. Glue the pieces of broken glass onto the line drawing. A mosaic picture will be created. Do not leave spaces between the glass. You can leave the background empty. Let dry completely before you continue to step 3.

3. Use the permanent magic markers to color in the glass, flames, and star.

OBJECTIVES: To learn the skill of bookbinding.
To create a *Sefer Hachayim*, using photos and pictures.

MATERIALS: Sheets of eight-and-a-half-by-eleven-inch paper, strong white thread, needle, piece of cardboard nine-by-eleven-and-a-half inches, scissors, piece of contact paper ten-by-twelve-and-a-half inches, glue, magic markers, photos, magazines.

DIRECTIONS:

1. To make the book pages, fold a pile of paper in half. Press down firmly along the fold.

2. Open the pages and sew along the folded seam in small back stitches. Finish the thread by sewing in and out of a few stitches on the back of the booklet (see Figure A).

3. To make the cover, peel the backing off the contact paper and place it sticky-side up. Center the cardboard on the sticky paper. Press down.

4. Cut each corner of the sticky paper at an angle, slanting the scissors toward the corner of the cardboard (see Figure B).

5. Press the sticky paper onto the cardboard, one side at a time. (Figure C shows the cover with three sides down.)

6. Fold the cover in half. Use the back of the scissors to press firmly along the seam.

7. Spread glue on the face of the first page of the sewn book. Press the page onto the inside half of the cover. Repeat on the back page.

8. Fill the pages of the Book of Life with photos of your family and wishes for them for the year. Or cut out pictures from magazines that represent your wishes for yourself or the world. Use the markers to decorate the front of the book and each page.

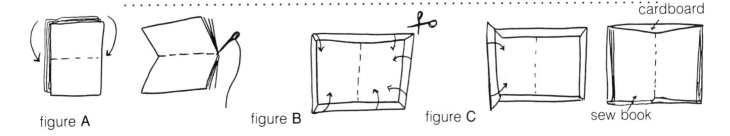

figure **A**   figure **B**   figure **C**   cardboard / sew book

Glossary

AFIKOMAN

A Greek word in origin (post-meal dessert), the *afikoman* is the middle of three matzot (unleavened bread) that are displayed on the Passover seder table. The *afikoman* is hidden as part of the orderly progress of the seder meal. It highlights the importance of matzah and provides a hide and seek experience for young people.

AM YISRAEL

The people of Israel (*Am Yisrael*) are an international family bound together by origin, experience, and values. The destiny of the Jewish people whether living in the State of Israel or in countries throughout the world exemplifies the miracle of survival.

ARON HAKODESH

During the biblical period it was reported that the ancient Hebrews carried the tablets of divinely revealed truth in a chest (box, ark). According to various rabbinic legends, both the ancient ark and the staves with which it was transported had significant power. The scrolls of Torah are safeguarded and displayed in a modern synagogue's ark (*Aron Hakodesh*).

BIBLE

The Bible (related terms include Torah, *TaNaCH*, Hebrew Scriptures, Five Books of Moses, Pentateuch, and *Chumash*) is the historical and spiritual diary of the Hebrew people; it is a handbook describing the origins, role models, and challenges of Jewish identity.

CHANUKAH

Chanukah is a winter festival celebrating Jewish pride, bravery, and self-respect. It recognizes the Maccabean battle and victory for religious freedom.

CHAROSET

A relishlike mixture of apples, figs, nuts, wine, dates, and spices used during the Passover seder to symbolize the mortar the biblical Hebrews were forced to prepare while firing bricks as slaves in Egypt. It is eaten in combination with bitter herbs.

COUNTING THE OMER

An *omer* is a measure of barley. During the biblical period, the measured technique of counting the *omer* (*sefirat ha'omer*) was used to count the days between the festivals of Passover and Shavuot; this gesture symbolizes the move from the freedom resulting from the Exodus out of Egyptian slavery to the freedom granted with the acceptance of Torah truths.

CREATION

Light is the initiating act of divine creation, according to the first chapter of the biblical Book of Genesis. Light symbolizes the move from darkness and chaos into a world of order and potential.

ERUV

At times like the Sabbath, Jewish law establishes boundaries that designate areas in which travel and the carrying of objects are allowed. When more than one area or domain is blended (the placement of food can qualify a locale as a new point from which to measure new and extended boundaries), an *eruv* has been created.

FAMILY

Mishpachah is the Hebrew term for family. Jewish families of every size and description have always served as the primary settings for Jewish education and experience.

HAVDALAH

The Sabbath is interpreted in classic Jewish writings as an ever-repeated experience of the messianic era. It is the pristine example of sacred time. When the Sabbath gives way—after sunset on Saturday evening—to the everyday week, its farewell is recognized by the ceremony of Havdalah (to make a distinction or separation). Reciting a blessing prior to drinking wine from a Kiddush cup highlights the sweetness of Shabbat. Smelling spices indicates the all-pervading impact of the Sabbath on the very soul of an individual. Lighting a twisted candle of many wicks symbolizes the responsibility of each Jew for every Jew and the unity of all humanity.

HEBREW

Known as the holy (unique) language, Hebrew is not only the historic language of Jewish study and prayer but the official means of communication in the State of Israel.

HISTORY

An appreciation for the past as related to Jewish life and lore is considered a requisite for a Jew's finding meaning in the present and focus for the future.

ISRAEL

Established as an independent nation in 1948, the State of Israel reflects both the Bible's identification of a special land for a special people and the yearning of Jews for a safe homeland.

JEWISH NOTABLES

Throughout Jewish history—from the biblical period to the present—members of the Jewish community personify the values of Judaism and contribute to the survival of the Jewish people. Moses, Theodor Herzl, Golda Meir, and Yitzhak Perlman are among such individuals.

KERIAH

According to a biblical narrative (II Samuel 13:31), King David tears his clothes upon hearing a report of the death of his son Absalom. Thus, for many members of the Jewish community, the tearing of a garment or the wearing of a small piece of cloth that has been torn still dramatizes one's feelings when confronted with the death of a loved one.

KRISTALLNACHT

This day of solemn commemoration marks the beginning of the Nazis' active and public destruction of Jews and the Jewish community—smashing the windows of shops owned by Jewish merchants, book burnings, beatings, and synagogue desecrations.

LAG BA'OMER

This festival indicates the thirty-third day of a period of seven weeks that serve to bridge Passover and Shavuot, relating the themes of freedom and revelation. Lag Ba'omer is often thought of as a students' holiday.

LECHAYIM

Hebrew for the toast "to life!" the expression *lechayim* asserts the centrality of living and enjoying a meaningful life. Using a cup of wine as a symbol of joy, the phrase *"lechayim"* is the proclamation of hope expressed at Sabbath and festival observances as well as other times when Jewish people wish to declare their happiness.

MATZAH

Matzah is a large round or square unleavened (no yeast) cracker prepared to replicate the quickly prepared "bread" the Jewish people ate when fleeing Egyptian slavery. This ancient symbol is central to the celebration of Passover and may well have ancient biblical origins predating the Exodus.

NER TAMID

An Eternal Light (*Ner Tamid*) is kept lit near a synagogue's ark, the repository for the scrolls of sacred teaching, the Torah. The *Ner Tamid* reflects the tradition of never extinguishing all the flames of the ancient candelabrum (menorah) housed in the biblical Temple of King Solomon.

NOAH'S ARK

The biblical Book of Genesis contains an allegorical-type narrative in which Noah, the personification of righteousness, becomes the hero in a disaster. The wickedness of the world and its inhabitants is "washed away" by a flood while the innocent animals are saved as voyagers on a seaworthy ark built by Noah and his family.

PASSOVER

A spring festival, Pesach (Hebrew name), celebrates the Exodus of the Hebrew people from their biblical enslavement by the Egyptian pharaoh. The origins of Passover include an ancient ritual involving the eating of unleavened bread.

PEOPLE

Described as the people of the Book and a unique (holy) people, Jews are members of a spiritual and cultural family governed by the principle: "Each Jew is responsible for every Jew."

PRAYER

The prayer book (siddur) is an orderly guide for a Jewish person's outreach to God through petition, thanksgiving, declaration, and recognition.

PURIM

A probable folk drama, Purim provides the Jewish people with a script in which hate is transformed into anti-Semitism, and personal integrity becomes the hallmark of a battle for Jewish survival.

ROSH HASHANAH

The Jewish New Year, Rosh Hashanah, is a fall holiday. It signals the advent of *Yamim Nora'im*, the "Days of Awe," which lasts until the end of Yom Kippur. The Jewish New Year celebrates the birthday of the world and designates an awe-inspiring period of introspection, humility, and renewal.

SEDER

The seder is a meal of prescribed order enabling its participants to experience the biblical Exodus from Egyptian slavery. Symbolic foods such as matzah (unleavened bread), saltwater (tears of slavery), *charoset* (mortarlike condiment), and parsley (springtime) are eaten in conjunction with the retelling of the Passover story using the haggadah—the Passover seder liturgy and guide.

SEFER HACHAYIM

Biblical and rabbinic texts allude to God's recording the destiny of every person during the period of Rosh Hashanah and Yom Kippur. This *Sefer Hachayim* (Book of Life) gives popular significance to these days of introspection, atonement, and resolution.

SHABBAT

Giving *tzedakah* (donating funds to help those in need); kindling candles with words of blessing; honoring one's family with expressions of praise; saluting creation, the Exodus from Egypt, and life by reciting the Kiddush prayer with a cup of wine; praising God for the sustenance of food in the words of *Hamotzi*—these are traditional aspects of a Jewish person's welcoming of the Sabbath.

SHALACH MANOT (MISHLO'ACH MANOT)

Preparing and sending sweets (*Shalach Manot*) to friends and neighbors during the holiday of Purim is a demonstration of the joyous victory of the Jews in the allegorical kingdom of Shushan (Susa) when threatened by the anti-Semitic Haman. Sharing the enjoyment of any festive Jewish celebration with the needy in one's community is considered a mitzvah (obligation) fulfilled.

SHALOM

Peace (shalom) indicates a state of being, interpersonal relationship, or international situation in which an absence of conflict is only one attribute. Shalom points to a time of fulfillment. It communicates a completed agenda in which all competition and tension are resolved.

SHAVUOT

The receipt of Torah as a gift of ennobling responsibilities for the Jewish people is the primary theme of Shavuot. Shavuot is one of the three pilgrim festivals—Sukot, Pesach, and Shavuot. At Shavuot the historic narrative of the Sinai experience is enriched by the reading of the biblical Book of Ruth, which relates a drama of choice and commitment.

SIMCHAT TORAH

Rejoicing in the weekly and ongoing study of Torah is the essence of a Jew's synagogue observance of Simchat Torah every fall. This festival identifies the Torah as the treasure of the Jewish people. It marks the congregation's completion of the biblical Book of Deuteronomy and the immediate repetition of the process by beginning the reading of the Book of Genesis.

SUKOT

Thanksgiving is the theme of Sukot. These temporary booths are a reminder of the way the Hebrew people would conduct the harvest during biblical times. Sukot celebrates the majesty of nature and features palm, willow, myrtle, and the *etrog* (lemonlike citrus) as its symbols.

SYNAGOGUE

A historic setting for prayer, study, and assembly, the synagogue continues to be the Jewish community's most authentic institution. Synagogue professionals—rabbis, cantors, educators, and administrators—enable congregations to continue the ceremonial, educational, and communal functions that began when the biblical Temple was in existence.

TISHAH BE'AV

This summer fast day serves as a memorial of national tragedies as well as periods of persecution experienced by the Jewish people: the destructions of the First and Second Temples, Bar Kochba's defeat, the expulsion from Spain, etc. The biblical Book of Lamentations is read along with other examples of mournful writings.

TU BISHVAT

Trees have played and continue to play a most significant role in the biblical lands in which the Jews have lived and currently live—most recently, in the State of Israel. Fruit, shade, shelter, and anti-soil erosion are some of the benefits celebrated on Tu-Bishvat—the New Year of the Trees.

USHPIZIN

During the festival of Sukot, a symbolic invitation to eat in the sukah (booth) is extended to the biblical ancestors of the Jewish people. These guests (*ushpizin*) validate the hospitable intent of the host/hostess and heighten the joy to be experienced in the traditional observance.

VALUES

Concepts such as peace (shalom), deeds of lovingkindness (*chesed*), pity on living creatures (*tza'ar ba'alei chayim*), truth (*emet*), etc., form a culture code through which the Jewish people enrich everyday life with the unique insights to be discovered in Torah and rabbinic literature.

YOM HA'ATZMA'UT

Israel's Independence Day celebrates the existence of the nation and its reflection of the Zionist ideal: a spiritual and political model of the justice, productivity, and security exemplified in a democracy whose history book is the Bible.

YOM HASHOAH

"Holocaust" is the word to label the World War II destruction of European Jewry as well as the planned annihilation of other peoples the Nazis had defined as inferior. Yom Hashoah is both a memorial to the six million Jews killed in death camps and a statement of commitment that the people of Israel will survive—regardless.

YOM KIPPUR

Yom Kippur, the Day of Atonement, is, in partnership with Rosh Hashanah, a time to admit one's unfulfilled promises and unethical behaviors in relation to others and to vow to improve oneself as well as the world.

YOTZER

The Hebrew term "*yotzer*" reflects the prayer book imagery of God as the creator of light. It helps the worshiper focus on the divine role in the natural wonders in which humans experience daily renewal.

RECIPES NEEDED FOR THE PROJECTS IN THIS BOOK

A. Play-Doh or Baker's Clay
This terrible-tasting dough is wonderful for sculpture. You shape it and bake it. (You could also just let it dry naturally.) The result is a very hard, permanent cookie or clay. But remember you can't eat it even if it looks "good enough to eat."

TO MAKE THE DOUGH:

Mix 1 cup of flour to
        1 cup of salt.
Add just a little water until the dough feels
        like modeling clay.
To color—add food coloring to the dough or
        wait and paint the dry sculpture
        with poster paints or watercolors.

TO SHAPE THE DOUGH:

Shape the dough as if it were clay. This dough can be rolled, cut, balled up, or pinched into shapes.

TO BAKE THE DOUGH:

Bake on a lightly greased cookie sheet (or one sprayed with nonstick cooking spray) in a 200°F. oven until very hard but not brown. The baking time depends on the size of the shapes.

B. Israeli Map Cookie Dough and Chanukah Mobile Dough
Any versatile sugar cookie recipe will work quite well, but my favorite is as follows:

¾ cup shortening
1 tsp. vanilla
1 cup sugar
2 eggs
2½ cups flour
1 tsp. baking powder
1 tsp. salt

Mix well shortening, sugar, eggs, and flavoring. Measure the flour and then sift into bowl. Blend flour, baking powder, and salt; stir in. Chill at least one hour. Preheat oven to 350°F. Roll out the chilled dough on a floured board. Cut the map of Israel from the dough with a sharp knife. Gently place the cookie on a lightly greased cookie sheet. Decorate the map according to the arts-and-crafts recipe.

C. Paint That "Sticks" to Metal and Smooth Surfaces
Adding a little dishwashing liquid to poster paint will allow the paint to adhere to metal and shiny, smooth surfaces.

D. "Snow Paint"
To create a "snowlike"-looking paint to use on black or blue construction paper all you need is Ivory Snow flakes and water.

TO MAKE THE SNOW PAINT:

Use a cup of Ivory Snow flakes. Add enough water to make it "paintable." (It should look like a thin yogurt.) Using a half-inch or larger paintbrush, dip the brush into this "snow paint" and paint on the dark construction paper to achieve the snow scenes.

E. Food Coloring Paint
To paint on cookies, such as the Israeli Map Cookie, you need to mix up a palette of colors using food coloring and egg yolks so a shiny "paint" will bake to a glossy finish.

TO MAKE THE FOOD COLORING PAINT:

4 egg yolks
red, yellow, blue, green food coloring
4 cups and 4 watercolor paintbrushes

Mix each color with the egg yolks until completely combined. Paint on the cookie dough as if it were regular paint. Make sure to use a thin paintbrush. Bake at 350°F. and make sure not to let it get brown. Brushes can easily be cleaned by washing with soap and water.

F. *Charoset* Recipes from around the World
Charoset represents the mortar the Hebrew slaves used in between the bricks in the building of the pyramids. This symbolic dish is prepared differently by Jewish communities all over the world. Why not try several next Passover.

Middle Eastern *Charoset*

2 oz. pine nuts (pignolias)
2 hard-boiled egg yolks
1 apple, grated
3 oz. almonds, ground
3½ oz. sugar
Juice and rind of 1 lemon
Shake of cinnamon
3 oz. raisins

Mash all ingredients or put into a food processor and blend into a well-mixed *charoset*.

Yemenite *Charoset*

30 dates, cut or chopped
20 dried figs, chopped
4 tbsps. sesame seeds

2 tsps. ginger powder
Red wine for moistening
Matzah meal as needed

Blend all fruits in a blender or food processor, mixed with the seasonings and wine, and if necessary add some matzah meal to thicken the *charoset*.

EVERYTHING YOU EVER WANTED TO KNOW ABOUT GLUE AND THEN SOME. . . .

A. HOW TO THIN THICKENED GLUE
Elmer's glue can be thinned with warm water. Add a few drops at a time, stirring until the consistency is right.

Rubber cement can be thinned by using rubber cement solvent. This can be bought in any arts-and-crafts store. Make sure to thin the glue in a well-ventilated room.

Paste-type glue can be thinned as you would Elmer's glue, using warm drops of water.

B. THE BEST TYPE OF GLUE TO USE WHEN. . .
Paper: Rubber cement, paper "liquid" glue from a tube.

Wood: Carpenter's glue (made by Elmer's), Elmer's glue, or Crazy Glue (used only with parental guidance).

Fabric: A "marshmallow-type" of glue. Tacky Glue is one brand; Sobo is another. They can be found in any arts-and-crafts store.

Papier-Mâché: Elmer's glue or Tacky Glue is fine.

Yarn, Wool, Thread: Elmer's glue or Tacky Glue.

Foil or Metal: Tacky Glue is best.

C. HOW TO MAKE GLUE IN A PINCH
An easy glue to make in a pinch is with flour and water. Add three tablespoons of flour to several drops of warm water. Mix until the consistency of heavy cream. Then use as you would Elmer's glue.

Another type of glue to make in a pinch is with wallpaper paste and water. Just follow the directions on the box or bag of wallpaper paste and glue as you would with Elmer's glue.

BASIC INFORMATION ON COMMON SUPPLIES USED IN ARTS AND CRAFTS

ITEM	THINNER AND CLEANER	FOR USE ON/FOR	NO. OF COATS	COMMENTS
Shellac	Alcohol	Wood, paper, clay	2	Use white shellac. Finish is waterproof. Fumes are toxic.
Enamel paint	Turpentine	Wood, paper, metal	1 or 2	Mix thoroughly.
Tempera paint	Water	Wood, paper, clay	1 or 2	Bright opaque paint. One color covers another.
Watercolor paint	Water	Wood, paper	1	Transparent colors. Brush strokes show.
Finger paint	Water	Shelf paper Butcher paper	—	Messy but fun. Good for textures.
Milk-Base glue (Elmer's)	Water	Any porous surface	—	Dries clear.
Library paste	Water	Paper	—	Dries opaque white.
Rubber cement	Solvent (benzol)	Paper	—	Tendency to bleed through paper; can be rolled off when dry.
Laundry starch	Water	Cloth, string	—	Liquid is best.
Wax	Brown bag over wax then iron off.	Candles, wax-resist paintings	—	Beeswax is easy to roll into a candle (or braid).
Clay (hardening type)	Soap and water	Sculpture, ritual objects, puppet heads, beads	—	Keep clay moist with a wet towel.
Play-Doh	Nail polish remover	Sculpture, beads	—	Keep sealed to prevent drying.
Flour dough	Water (while still soft)	Sculpture, beads	—	Bake to harden.
Papier-Mâché	Water	Puppet heads, sculpture	—	Add two aspirin to the water to prevent molds.

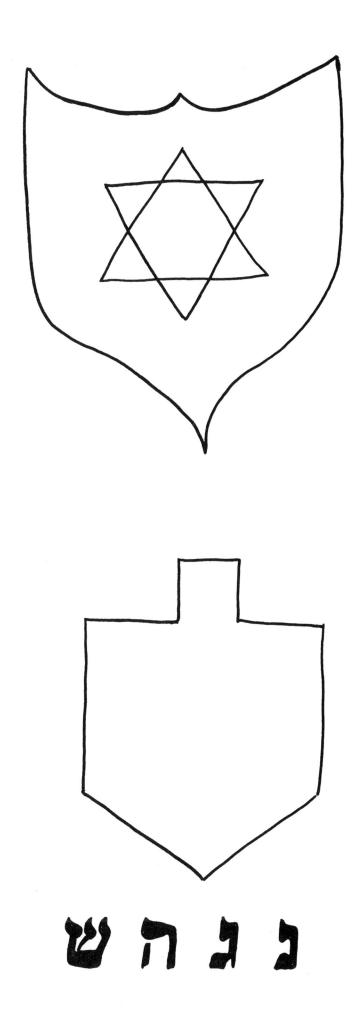

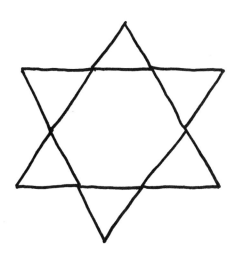

נ ג ה ש

ISRAELI MAP COOKIE

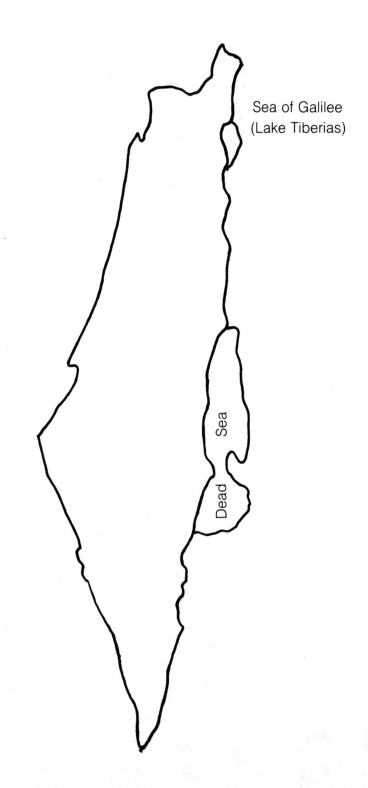

Sea of Galilee
(Lake Tiberias)

Dead Sea

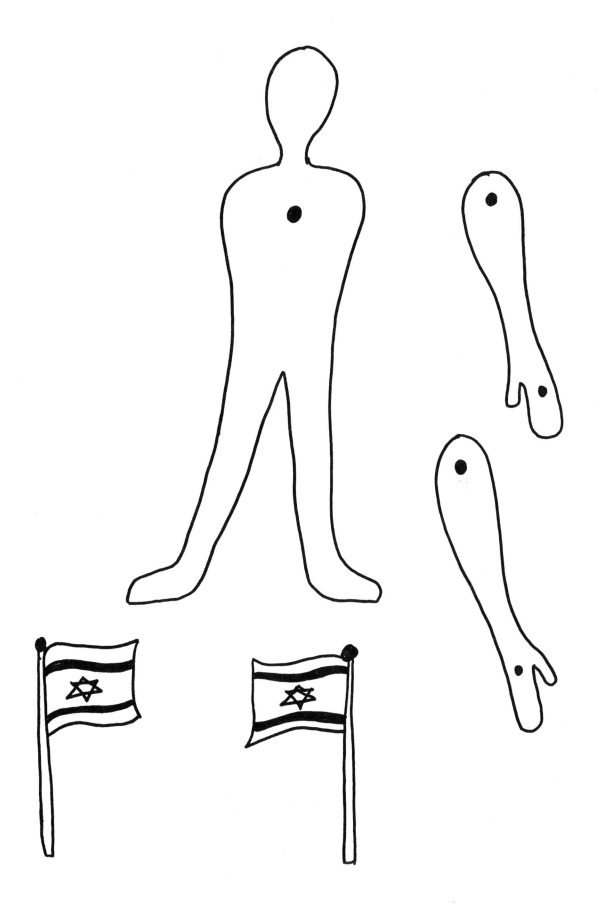